QUICK A... MICROWAVE COOKING FOR ONE

Rena Croft

foulsham

LONDON . NEW YORK . TORONTO . SYDNEY

foulsham

The Publishing House, Bennetts Close,
Cippenham, Berks SL1 5AP

ISBN   0-572-02151-8

Printed in Great Britain by
Cox & Wyman Ltd,
Reading.

CONTENTS

INTRODUCTION

Cooking for one can be a real chore – especially after a long day at work. How often do you just reach for the nearest can or opt for a sandwich? It is all too tempting. But with just a little more thought, you can prepare simple and nutritious meals for one with the help of your microwave. That way you can add variety and interest into your diet.

The recipes in this book are designed to be quick and easy and designed for one. That way you do not have the trouble of working out how long the meal will take to prepare, or calculate a quarter of the quantities in an ordinary cookery book. Ingredients have been selected so they use a range of meats and vegetables in cuts and quantities which are easy to buy on a small scale. The recipes have also been written as simply as possible – minimising confusing instructions and washing up.

If you do want to cook for more than one, simply increase the quantities. If you double the quantity, increase the cooking times by about half as much again and check the food carefully until it is cooked correctly. It is always better to undercook in a microwave then return the food for a few more seconds or minutes. If you overcook, you may spoil the dish.

Add a little imagination and start to enjoy interesting meals from your microwave.

Tips On Microwaving
For One

1. Plan in advance to avoid extra shopping trips.

2. Use individual – sized microwave cookware for best results. Buy some cookware you can use for cooking and serving to save washing up.

3. Freeze meat and other items in individual quantities. Freeze stock in ice cube trays ready for use. Keep a stock of pitta breads, rolls, sticks of cream and a few frozen vegetables.

4. Cook dishes in larger quantities and freeze in individual portions.

5. Be careful not to over season small quantities.

6. Always undercook and check the food. If overcooked, it will spoil.

7. Arrange foods with the thickest portions to the outside.

8. Chop fresh herbs then freeze in small quantities ready for use straight from the freezer.

Notes For Cooks

1. Follow one set of measurements only, do not mix metric, Imperial or American.

2. Eggs are size 2.

3. Wash fresh produce before preparation.

4. Spoon measurements are level.

5. A tablespoon is 15 ml; a teaspoon is 5 ml.

6. Adjust seasoning and strongly flavoured ingredients, such as onions and garlic, to suit your own taste.

7. If you substitute dried for fresh herbs, use only half the amount specified.

8. All the recipes serve 1 unless otherwise specified.

9. Times are based on a 600 watt microwave oven. Cooking times in a microwave vary depending on the temperature of the food when cooking starts, the size and shape of the container, and so on. Always undercook rather than overcook and test the food regularly during cooking.

10. Preparation times include both preparation and cooking and are approximate.

Soups

ASPARAGUS SOUP

ingredients	Metric	Imperial	American
Butter or margarine	15 ml	1 tbsp	1 tbsp
Asparagus, cut into chunks	100 g	4 oz	¼ lb
Spring onion (scallion), chopped	1	1	1
Cornflour (cornstarch)	15 ml	1 tbsp	1 tbsp
Milk	250 ml	8 fl oz	1 cup
Salt and freshly ground black pepper			
Double cream	45 ml	3 tbsp	3 tbsp

method

1. Place the butter, asparagus and spring onion in a large bowl, cover and microwave on High for 3-4 minutes until tender, stirring once or twice during cooking.

2. Mix the cornflour with a little of the milk then stir into the asparagus with the remaining milk. Season with salt and pepper, cover and microwave on High for 3 minutes, stirring occasionally.

3. Purée the soup in a food processor and stir in the cream. Reheat if necessary, but do not allow the soup to boil.

 8-10 min Preparation time

BROCCOLI SOUP

ingredients	Metric	Imperial	American
Spring onion (scallion), chopped	1	1	1
Butter or margarine	15 ml	1 tbsp	1 tbsp
Plain (all-purpose) flour	10 ml	2 tsp	2 tsp
Chicken stock	150 ml	¼ pt	⅔ cup
Broccoli florets, frozen or blanched, chopped	50 g	2 oz	⅛ lb
Pinch of grated nutmeg			
Salt and freshly ground black pepper			
Milk	75 ml	5 tbsp	5 tbsp

method

1. Place the spring onion and butter or margarine in a bowl and microwave on High for 1 minute.

2. Stir in all the remaining ingredients except the milk and microwave on High for 3-4 minutes, stirring once or twice.

3. Purée in a food processor, stir in the milk and season with salt and pepper. Microwave on High for 1 minute, stirring once.

4. Leave to stand for 1 minute before serving.

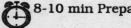 8-10 min Preparation time

SPANISH BEAN SOUP

ingredients	Metric	Imperial	American
Canned chick peas (garbanzos), drained	100 g	4 oz	¼ lb
Cooked ham, cubed	50 g	2 oz	⅛ lb
Smoked bacon, diced	50 g	2 oz	⅛ lb
Braising steak, cut into strips	50 g	2 oz	⅛ lb
Tomato purée (paste)	15 ml	1 tbsp	1 tbsp
Spring onion (scallion), chopped	1	1	1
Bay leaf	½	½	½
Potato, cubed	1	1	1

method

1. Stir all the ingredients into a casserole and almost cover with water. Microwave on High for 10-15 minutes until the potatoes are tender and the soup well heated through.

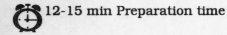 12-15 min Preparation time

CREAM OF MUSHROOM SOUP

ingredients	Metric	Imperial	American
Butter or margarine	15 ml	1 tbsp	1 tbsp
Shallot, finely chopped	1	1	1
Mushrooms, sliced	50 g	2 oz	1 cup
Plain (all-purpose) flour	10 ml	2 tsp	2 tsp
Vegetable stock	120 ml	4 fl oz	½ cup
Milk	120 ml	4 fl oz	½ cup
Salt and freshly ground black pepper			
Single (light) cream	15 ml	1 tbsp	1 tbsp
Chopped fresh parsley	5 ml	1 tsp	1 tsp

method

1. Place the butter or margarine, shallot and mushrooms in a bowl and microwave on High for 2-3 minutes until soft.

2. Stir in the flour and microwave on High for 30 seconds.

3. Stir in the stock and milk, season with salt and pepper and microwave on High for 3-4 minutes.

4. Purée the soup in a food processor or blender.

5. Stir in the cream and microwave on High for 30 seconds to reheat. Serve sprinkled with parsley.

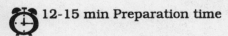 12-15 min Preparation time

RICH ONION SOUP

ingredients	Metric	Imperial	American
Butter or margarine	15 ml	1 tbsp	1 tbsp
Onions, finely chopped	100 g	4 oz	¼ lb
Plain (all-purpose) flour	5 ml	1 tsp	1 tsp
Beef stock	150 ml	¼ pt	⅔ cup
Salt and freshly ground black pepper			
Milk	60 ml	4 tbsp	4 tbsp
Chopped fresh parsley	5 ml	1 tsp	1 tsp

method

1. Place the butter or margarine and onions in a casserole and microwave on High for 2 minutes until soft, stirring once during cooking.

2. Stir in the flour, then blend in the stock and season with salt and pepper. Microwave on High for 3-5 minutes.

3. Purée the soup in a food processor or blender.

4. Meanwhile, microwave the milk on High for 45 seconds. Stir it into the onion mixture and microwave on High for about 1minute. Serve sprinkled with parsley.

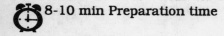 8-10 min Preparation time

Parsnip and Leek Soup

ingredients	Metric	Imperial	American
Parsnip, grated	1	1	1
Leek, sliced	1	1	1
Chicken stock	45 ml	3 tbsp	3 tbsp
Pinch of ground mace			
Salt and freshly ground black pepper			
Milk	120 ml	4 fl oz	½ cup
Pinch of chopped fresh chives			

method

1. Place the parsnip, leek, stock, mace, salt and pepper in a bowl and stir well. Cover and microwave on High for 3-4 minutes.

2. Stir well then cover and cook for a further 3-4 minutes until the vegetables are soft.

3. Stir in the milk then purée in a food processor or blender.

4. Return to the microwave and microwave on High for 30-50 seconds until heated through. Serve sprinkled with chives.

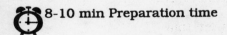 8-10 min Preparation time

PEPPER AND CHICKEN SOUP WITH RICE

ingredients	Metric	Imperial	American
Small red (bell) pepper, chopped	1	1	1
Small onion, chopped	1	1	1
Oil	5 ml	1 tsp	1 tsp
Chicken stock	300 ml	½ pt	1¼ cups
Long-grain rice	30 ml	2 tbsp	2 tbsp
Salt and freshly ground black pepper			

method

1. Put the pepper, onion and oil in a casserole dish, cover and microwave on High for 2 minutes, stirring once.

2. Add the stock, cover and microwave on High for 3-5 minutes until hot.

3. Stir in the rice, salt and pepper, cover and microwave on High for 5-7 minutes until the rice is cooked, stirring several times during cooking.

4. Cover and leave to stand for 2 minutes before serving.

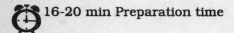 16-20 min Preparation time

PRAWN AND TARRAGON SOUP

ingredients	Metric	Imperial	American
Butter or margarine	*10 ml*	*2 tsp*	*2 tsp*
Button mushrooms, sliced	*25 g*	*1 oz*	*½ cup*
Small courgette (zucchini), cut into strips	*1*	*1*	*1*
Spring onion (scallion), sliced	*1*	*1*	*1*
Chopped fresh parsley	*5 ml*	*1 tsp*	*1 tsp*
Condensed chicken soup	*75 ml*	*5 tbsp*	*5 tbsp*
Water	*75 ml*	*5 tbsp*	*5 tbsp*
Dry white wine	*15 ml*	*1 tbsp*	*1 tbsp*
Pinch of dried tarragon			
Peeled prawns (shrimp)	*50 g*	*2 oz*	*½ cup*
Salt and freshly ground black pepper			

method

1. Put the butter or margarine, mushrooms, courgette and spring onion in a casserole and microwave on High for 1-2 minutes until just soft, stirring once during cooking.

2. Stir in the remaining ingredients except the prawns, salt and pepper and microwave on High for 2-3 minutes until boiling.

3. Stir in the prawns and season with salt and pepper. Microwave on Medium for 1-2 minutes until heated through.

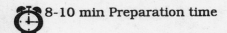 8-10 min Preparation time

POTATO AND CHEESE SOUP

ingredients	Metric	Imperial	American
Potato, cubed	1	1	1
Small carrot, chopped	1	1	1
Celery stick, chopped	½	½	½
Spring onion (scallion), chopped	1	1	1
Chicken stock	75 ml	5 tbsp	5 tbsp
Salt and freshly ground black pepper			
Milk	75 ml	5 tbsp	5 tbsp
Cheddar cheese, grated	50 g	2 oz	½ cup

method

1. Put the potato, carrot, celery, spring onion, half the stock, salt and pepper into a casserole, cover and microwave on High for 5-8 minutes until the vegetables are tender, stirring once during cooking.

2. Purée the mixture in a food processor then return it to the casserole.

3. Blend in the remaining stock and the milk to make the consistency you prefer. Stir in the cheese, cover and microwave on High for about 1 minute until the cheese melts.

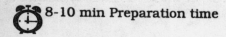 8-10 min Preparation time

SWEETCORN SOUP

ingredients	Metric	Imperial	American
Butter or margarine	10 ml	2 tsp	2 tsp
Small onion, finely chopped	½	½	½
Bacon rasher (slice), rinded and chopped	1	1	1
Cornflour (cornstarch)	5 ml	1 tsp	1 tsp
Milk	45 ml	3 tbsp	3 tbsp
Sweetcorn kernels	50 g	2 oz	½ cup
Chicken stock, hot	75 ml	5 tbsp	5 tbsp
Salt and freshly ground black pepper			
Single (light) cream	15 ml	1 tbsp	1 tbsp
Spring onion (scallion), chopped	½	½	½

method

1. Place the butter or margarine, onion and bacon in a bowl and microwave on High for 1 minute.

2. Blend the cornflour with the milk then stir into the bowl and microwave on High for 1-2 minutes, stirring once during cooking.

3. Whisk the mixture well then stir in the sweetcorn and stock and microwave on High for 1-2 minutes, stirring once during cooking. Season to taste. Stir in the cream and serve garnished with spring onion.

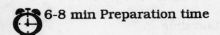 6-8 min Preparation time

TOMATO SOUP

ingredients	Metric	Imperial	American
Butter or margarine	10 ml	2 tsp	2 tsp
Small onion, chopped	½	½	½
Celery stick, chopped	½	½	½
Tomatoes, skinned and chopped	225 g	8 oz	½ lb
Plain (all-purpose) flour	10 ml	2 tsp	2 tsp
Chicken stock, hot	150 ml	¼ pt	⅔ cup
Tomato purée (paste)	10 ml	2 tsp	2 tsp
Salt and freshly ground black pepper			
Pinch of chopped fresh basil			
Double (heavy) cream, whipped	30 ml	2 tbsp	2 tbsp
Pinch of chopped fresh parsley			

method

1. Put the butter or margarine in a bowl and microwave on High for 20 seconds until melted. Add the onion and celery and microwave on High for 3 minutes.

2. Add the tomatoes and microwave on High for 1 minute.

3. Stir in the flour, stock and tomato purée. Microwave on High for 3 minutes.

4. Season with salt, pepper and basil. Swirl in the cream and serve garnished with parsley.

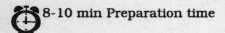 8-10 min Preparation time

CREAMY SALMON SOUP

ingredients	Metric	Imperial	American
Butter or margarine	15 ml	1 tbsp	1 tbsp
Button mushrooms, sliced	2	2	2
Spring onion (scallion), chopped	1	1	1
Pinch of dried tarragon			
Plain (all-purpose) flour		10 ml	2 tsp2 tsp
Chopped fresh parsley	5 ml	1 tsp	1 tsp
Dijon mustard	2.5 ml	½ tsp	½ tsp
Salt and freshly ground black pepper			
Milk	120 ml	4 fl oz	½ cup
Canned salmon, drained and flaked	50 g	2 oz	⅓ cup

method

1. Put the butter or margarine, mushrooms, spring onion and tarragon in a casserole, cover and microwave on High for 1-2 minutes until the onion is soft.

2. Stir in the flour, parsley, mustard, salt and pepper then blend in the milk. Microwave, uncovered, on Medium for 3-4 minutes until the mixture thickens and bubbles.

3. Stir in the salmon and microwave on Medium for 30 seconds until heated through. Adjust the thickness with a little more milk or cream, if necessary.

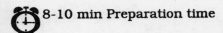 8-10 min Preparation time

VEGETABLE SOUP WITH CHEESE

Ingredients	Metric	Imperial	American
Oil	5 ml	1 tsp	1 tsp
Carrot, thinly sliced	½	½	½
Onion, thinly sliced	½	½	½
Celery stick, thinly sliced	½	½	½
Vegetable stock	250 ml	8 fl oz	1 cup
Salt and freshly ground black pepper			
Canned chopped tomatoes	50 g	2 oz	¼ cup
Grated Parmesan cheese	15 ml	1 tbsp	1 tbsp
Chopped fresh parsley	10 ml	2 tsp	2 tsp

method

1. Place the oil, carrot, onion and celery in a casserole dish and microwave on High for 1 minute.

2. Stir in the stock and season with salt and pepper. Microwave on High for 8-9 minutes, stirring twice during cooking.

3. Stir in the tomatoes and microwave on High for 4-5 minutes, stirring once during cooking. Serve sprinkled with Parmesan and parsley.

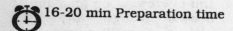 16-20 min Preparation time

BORTSCH

ingredients	Metric	Imperial	American
Raw beetroot (red beets) grated	75 g	3 oz	6 tbsp
Water	150 ml	¼ pt	⅔ cup
Pinch of sugar			
Lemon juice	10 ml	2 tsp	2 tsp
Salt and freshly ground black pepper			
Soured (dairy sour) cream	30 ml	2 tbsp	2 tbsp

method

1. Wash and peel the beetroot and grate it coarsely. Place it in a casserole dish with the water, sugar and lemon juice and season to taste with salt and pepper.

2. Cover and microwave on High for 3-4 minutes until the beetroot is tender, stirring once during cooking.

3. Leave to cool then chill for several hours. Serve garnished with soured cream.

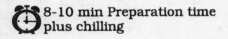 8-10 min Preparation time plus chilling

VICHYSSOISE

ingredients	Metric	Imperial	American
Potato, peeled and thinly sliced	1	1	1
Chicken stock	30 ml	2 tbsp	2 tbsp
Butter or margarine	15 ml	1 tbsp	1 tbsp
Milk	120 ml	4 fl oz	½ cup
Leek, finely chopped	½	½	½
Salt and freshly ground black pepper			
Chopped fresh chives	5 ml	1 tsp	1 tsp

method

1. Put the potato and stock in a casserole dish, cover and microwave on High for 4-5 minutes until the potato is soft, stirring once or twice during cooking.

2. Add half the butter or margarine and a little of the milk and mash the potato until smooth.

3. Put the remaining butter or margarine and the leek into a bowl, cover and microwave on High for 1-2 minutes until the leek is soft, stirring once. Mix the leeks, the remaining milk, salt and pepper into the potatoes, adding a little more milk if necessary to reach the desired consistency.

4. Leave to cool then chill before serving garnished with chives.

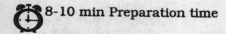 8-10 min Preparation time

STARTERS & SNACKS

HOT SPICED GRAPEFRUIT

ingredients	Metric	Imperial	American
Large grapefruit	½	½	½
Butter or margarine	25 g	1 oz	2 tbsp
Soft brown sugar	25 g	1 oz	2 tbsp
Pinch of ground cinnamon			
Glacé cherry		1	11
Fresh mint sprig	1	1	1

method

1. Cut through the grapefruit between the membranes and flesh to release the segments.

2. Mix together the butter or margarine and sugar to a paste and work in a little cinnamon to taste. Spread the mixture over the grapefruit.

3. Microwave on High for 1 minute until the butter mixture melts. Garnish with the cherry and mint and serve immediately.

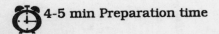 4-5 min Preparation time

PITTA SNACKS

ingredients	Metric	Imperial	American
Pitta bread	1	1	1
Olive oil	5 ml	1 tsp	1 tsp
Canned passata (sieved tomatoes)	45 ml	3 tbsp	3 tbsp
Button mushrooms, sliced	2	2	2
Mortadella slice, chopped	1	1	1
Pinch of dried oregano			
Mozzarella cheese, shredded	50 g	2 oz	1/4 cup

method

1. Sliced the pitta in half horizontally. Brush the cut sides with olive oil and spread with the passata.

2. Sprinkle the mushrooms, mortadella and oregano over the surfaces and cover with the cheese.

3. Microwave on Medium for 45-60 seconds until the cheese has melted.

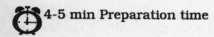 4-5 min Preparation time

PRAWN DIP

ingredients	Metric	Imperial	American
Spring onion (scallion), chopped	1	1	1
Celery stick, chopped	½	½	½
Butter or margarine	5 ml	1 tsp	1 tsp
Peeled prawns (shrimp)	50 g	2 oz	½ cup
Hard-boiled (hard-cooked) egg, chopped	½	½	½
Pinch of made mustard			
Pinch of cayenne pepper			
Cottage cheese	50 g	2 oz	¼ cup
Milk	30 ml	2 tbsp	2 tbsp

method

1. Put the spring onion, celery and butter or margarine into a bowl and microwave on High for 30 seconds until the celery is tender but still crisp.

2. Stir in the prawns, egg, mustard and cayenne pepper.

3. In a blender or food processor, blend the cottage cheese and milk until smooth. Stir into the prawn mixture.

4. Leave to cool then chill before serving with crackers or crudités.

4-5 min Preparation time
plus chilling

AVOCADO DIP

ingredients	Metric	Imperial	American
Bacon rasher (slice), rinded	1	1	1
Ripe avocado	1/2	1/2	1/2
Lemon juice	5 ml	1 tsp	1 tsp
Pinch of chilli powder			
Salt and freshly ground black pepper			
Tomato, skinned and chopped	1/4	1/4	1/4

method

1. Arrange the bacon on a layer of kitchen pepper, cover with kitchen paper and microwave on High for 1-2 minutes until crisp. Leave to stand for 1-2 minutes.

2. Mash the avocado flesh with the lemon juice, chilli powder, salt and pepper.

3. Crumble the bacon into the mixture and stir well.

4. Stir in the tomato and serve with tortilla chips or crackers.

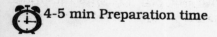 4-5 min Preparation time

BACON AND CHEESE DIP

ingredients	Metric	Imperial	American
Bacon rashers (slices), rinded	4	4	4
Unsalted butter or margarine	50 g	2 oz	¼ cup
Cream cheese	50 g	2 oz	¼ cup
Gruyère cheese, grated	50 g	2 oz	½ cup
Pinch of paprika			
Small spring onion (scallion), chopped	1	1	1
Salt and freshly ground black pepper			

method

1. Put the bacon in a casserole dish, cover and microwave on High for 4-5 minutes until crisp.

2. Drain on kitchen paper then crumble and set a side.

3. Mix the butter or margarine and cream cheese. Microwave on Medium for 20 seconds until soft.

4. Mix in the crumbled bacon, gruyère cheese, paprika and spring onion. Season with salt and pepper. Serve with crackers or crudits.

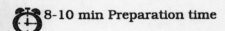 8-10 min Preparation time

SMOKED OYSTER DIP

ingredients	Metric	Imperial	American
Celery stick, finely chopped	½	½	½
Spring onion (scallion), chopped	1	1	1
Butter or margarine	5 ml	1 tsp	1 tsp
Canned smoked oysters, drained and chopped	50 g	2 oz	⅛ lb
Soured (dairy sour) cream	30 ml	2 tbsp	2 tbsp
Natural (plain) yoghurt	30 ml	2 tbsp	2 tbsp
Mayonnaise	15 ml	1 tbsp	1 tbsp
Chopped fresh parsley	5 ml	1 tsp	1 tsp
Squeeze of lemon juice			
Freshly ground black pepper			

method

1. Put the celery, spring onion and butter or margarine in a bowl and microwave on High for 1-2 minutes until tender but still crisp.

2. Stir in the remaining ingredients and serve at room temperature or chilled.

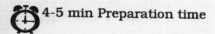 4-5 min Preparation time

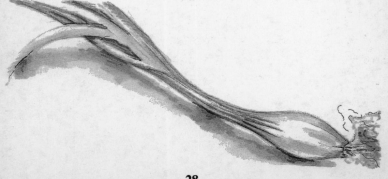

CHICKEN LIVER PATE

ingredients	Metric	Imperial	American
Spring onion (scallion), chopped	1	1	1
Garlic clove, crushed	½	½	½
Butter or margarine	15 ml	1 tbsp	1 tbsp
Chicken livers	75 g	3 oz	scant ¼ lb
Salt and freshly ground black pepper			
Pinch of ground mace			
Brandy	5 ml	1 tsp	1 tsp
Lemon slices			

method

1. Put the spring onion, garlic and butter or margarine in a bowl and microwave on High for 1½ minutes, stirring once.

2. Add the chicken livers and cook for 2 minutes, stirring twice.

3. Cool for 5 minutes then season with salt, pepper and mace. Stir in the brandy then rub through a sieve.

4. Press into an individual dish and smooth the top. Garnish with a slice of lemon and serve cold with toast.

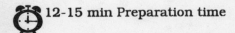 12-15 min Preparation time

SMOKED HADDOCK PATE

Serves 4: freeze in individual portions before garnishing

ingredients	Metric	Imperial	American
Smoked haddock fillets	150 g	6 oz	3/8 lb
Butter or margarine	25 g	1 oz	2 tbsp
Lemon juice	10 ml	2 tsp	2 tsp
Garlic clove, crushed	1	1	1
Brandy	15 ml	1 tsp	1 tbsp
Few drops of tabasco sauce			
Single (light) cream	30 ml	2 tbsp	2 tbsp
Lemon, thinly sliced	1/2	1/2	1/2

method

1. Place the haddock on a plate, dot with butter or margarine, cover and microwave on High for 5 minutes.

2. Remove the skin and any bones. Purée in a food processor or rub through a sieve.

3. Add the lemon juice, garlic, brandy, tabasco sauce and cream and blend until smooth.

4. Press into individual dishes and chill. Garnish with lemon slices and serve cold with toast.

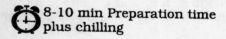 8-10 min Preparation time
plus chilling

MACKEREL POT

ingredients	Metric	Imperial	American
Small smoked mackerel fillet	1	1	1
Butter or margarine	5 ml	1 tsp	1 tsp
Plain (all-purpose) flour	5 ml	1 tsp	1 tsp
Milk	75 ml	5 tbsp	5 tbsp
Cheddar cheese, grated	15 ml	1 tbsp	1 tbsp
Salt and freshly ground black pepper			
Pinch of mustard powder			

method

1. Remove the skin from the fillets and flake the flesh.

2. Put the butter or margarine in a bowl and microwave on High for 20 seconds. Stir in the flour and milk and microwave on High for 1 minute. Whisk well.

3. Fold in the fish, most of the cheese, the salt, pepper and mustard and place in an individual dish. Sprinkle with the reserved cheese and microwave on High for 1 minute until thecheese melts. Serve hot with toast.

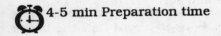 4-5 min Preparation time

LEEK AND NUT PANCAKES

ingredients	Metric	Imperial	American
Batter:			
Plain (all-purpose) flour	25 g	1 oz	¼ cup
Pinch of salt			
Milk	75 ml	5 tbsp	5 tbsp
Egg yolk	1	1	1
Few drops of vegetable oil			
Filling:			
Vegetable oil	5 ml	1 tsp	1 tsp
Small leek, chopped	1	1	1
Soured (dairy sour) cream	45 ml	3 tbsp	3 tbsp
Walnuts, chopped	25 g	1 oz	¼ cup
Cornflour (cornstarch)	5 ml	1 tsp	1 tsp
Milk	10 ml	2 tsp	2 tsp
Salt and freshly ground black pepper			
To garnish:			
Grated Parmesan cheese	15 ml	1 tbsp	1 tbsp

method

1. Mix the flour and salt then whisk in the remaining batter ingredients until smooth. Leave to stand for 1 hour.

2. Lightly oil a pancake pan and heat on a conventional oven. Pour in about half the batter, swirl around and cook for about 2 minutes. Turn and cook the other side. Make a second pancake in the same way.

3. Place the oil and leek in a bowl and microwave on High for 1 minute. Leave to cool slightly. Add the soured cream and walnuts. Mix the cornflour with the milk and stir into the mixture with the salt and pepper. Microwave on High for 1 minute until thick, stirring once.

4. Stuff the pancakes with the mixture, arrange on a plate and microwave on High for 1-2 minutes. Serve garnished with Parmesan.

 8-10 min Preparation time

SPINACH FLORENTINE

ingredients	Metric	Imperial	American
Spinach	50 g	2 oz	⅛ lb
Butter or margarine	15 ml	1 tbsp	1 tbsp
Plain (all-purpose) flour	15 ml	1 tbsp	1 tbsp
Milk	75 ml	5 tbsp	5 tbsp
Grated Cheddar cheese	30 ml	2 tbsp	2 tbsp
Egg	1	1	1
Pinch of grated nutmeg			
Salt and pepper			
Grated Parmesan cheese	10 ml	2 tsp	2 tsp

method

1. Wash the spinach and remove the stems. Place in a bowl, partially cover and microwave on High for 2 minutes. Squeeze out excess water and place on a greased individual dish.

2. Place the butter or margarine and flour in a jug and microwave on High for 30 seconds. Whisk in the milk and microwave on High for 1-2 minutes. Whisk until smooth and thick. Stir in the cheese.

3. Break the egg on to the spinach and season with nutmeg, salt and pepper. Pour over the cheese sauce and microwave on High for 2 minutes or until the eggs are just set. Garnish with Parmesan before serving.

 8-10 min Preparation time

PRAWN ROLL-UPS

ingredients	Metric	Imperial	American
Bacon rashers (slices), rinded and quartered	2	2	2
Large raw peeled prawns (shrimps), halved	4	4	4
Green (bell) pepper, cut into 8	1	1	1
Soy sauce	15 ml	1 tbsp	1 tbsp
Water	15 ml	1 tbsp	1 tbsp
Chilli sauce	15 ml	1 tbsp	1 tbsp
Redcurrant jelly	15 ml	1 tbsp	1 tbsp

method

1. Arrange the bacon on a plate lined with kitchen paper and cover with another sheet of kitchen paper. Microwave on High for about 2 minutes until lightly browned but not crisp.

2. Wrap each piece of bacon around a prawn and a piece of green pepper and secure with a cocktail stick (toothpick). Arrange in a dish.

3. Mix together the remaining ingredients and pour over the prawns. Cover and chill for several hours.

4. Microwave on High for 2-3 minutes until the prawns are cooked.

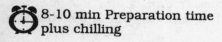 8-10 min Preparation time plus chilling

note

If you use cooked prawns, microwave for just 30-45 seconds until heated through.

CHEESEY BACON TWISTS

ingredients	Metric	Imperial	American
Garlic clove, halved	1	1	1
Bacon rashers (slices), rinded	2	2	2
Grissini (bread sticks)	2	2	2
Parmesan cheese, finely grated	30 ml	2 tbsp	2 tbsp
Salt and freshly ground black pepper			

method

1. Rub the cut side of the garlic over the bacon then twist the bacon in a spiral round the bread sticks.

2. Place on a plate covered with kitchen paper and microwave on High for 2-3 minutes until the bacon is crisp.

3. Season the cheese with salt and pepper in a bowl. Twist the bacon-wrapped bread sticks in the cheese until coated. Serve hot or cold.

 4-5 min Preparation time

SAUSAGE AND BACON ROLLS

ingredients	Metric	Imperial	American
Cocktail sausages	100 g	4 oz	¼ lb
Bacon rashers (slices), rinded	100 g	4 oz	¼ lb

method

1. Prick the sausages with a fork.

2. Stretch the bacon with the flat of a knife and cut into the same number of pieces as you have sausages.

3. Wrap the bacon strips around the sausages and arrange on a rack or plate. Microwave on High for 3-4 minutes, rearranging once or twice during cooking.

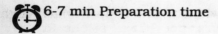 6-7 min Preparation time

DRUNKEN PRAWNS

ingredients	Metric	Imperial	American
Butter or margarine	15 ml	1 tbsp	1 tbsp
Spring onion (scallion), chopped	1	1	1
Peeled prawns (shrimp)	75 g	3 oz	scant ¼ lb
Double (heavy) cream	15 ml	1 tbsp	1 tbsp
Brandy	15 ml	1 tbsp	1 tbsp
Salt and freshly ground black pepper			

method

1. Place the butter or margarine in a bowl and microwave on High for 30 seconds until melted. Stir in the spring onion and microwave on High for 1 minute, stirring once.

2. Stir in the prawns, cover and microwave on High for 40 seconds.

3. Place the cream and brandy in a separate bowl and microwave on High for 20 seconds. Season with salt and pepper and spoon over the prawns. Serve hot with toast.

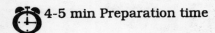 4-5 min Preparation time

CRAB ROUNDS

ingredients	Metric	Imperial	American
Crab meat	175 g	6 oz	⅜ lb
Spring onion (scallion), sliced	1	1	1
Mayonnaise	15 ml	1 tbsp	1 tbsp
Chopped fresh parsley	10 ml	2 tsp	2 tsp
Grated Cheddar cheese	30 ml	2 tbsp	2 tbsp
Melba toast rounds	8	8	8
Paprika			

method

1. Mix the crab meat, spring onion, mayonnaise and parsley in a small bowl. Stir in the cheese.

2. Line a plate with 2 layers of kitchen paper. Spoon the crab mixture on the toast rounds and arrange on the plate. Microwave on High for about 1 minute until the cheese melts, rearranging once during cooking.

3. Serve sprinkled with paprika.

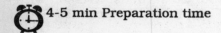 4-5 min Preparation time

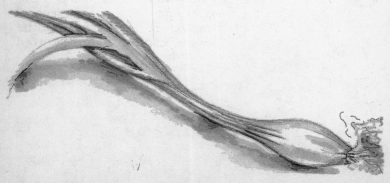

CHICKEN AND COURGETTE BOATS

ingredients	Metric	Imperial	American
Chicken breast	50 g	2 oz	⅛ lb
Pinch of dried tarragon			
Pinch of onion salt			
Flaked almonds	15 ml	1 tbsp	1 tbsp
Soured (dairy sour) cream	5 ml	1 tsp	1 tsp
Dijon mustard	2.5 ml	½ tsp	½ tsp
Few drops of tabasco sauce			
Salt and freshly ground black pepper			
Courgette (zucchini)	1	1	1
Small carrot, grated	1	1	1

method

1. Skin the chicken and place it in a baking dish. Sprinkle with tarragon and onion salt, cover with microwave film and microwave on Medium for 2-4 minutes until the chicken is no longer pink.

2. Chop or shred the chicken meat and mix with the remaining ingredients except the courgette and carrot.

3. Halve the courgette lengthways and scoop out the flesh to make a boat shape. Mix the courgette flesh with the chicken mixture and spoon into the courgette boats. Serve garnished with grated carrot.

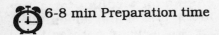 6-8 min Preparation time

Eggs & Cheese

EGGS WITH ANCHOVIES

ingredients	Metric	Imperial	American
Egg	1	1	1
Cream cheese	10 ml	2 tsp	2 tsp
Whipping (heavy) cream	75 ml	5 tbsp	5 tbsp
Few drops of lemon juice			
Anchovy fillets, drained and chopped	2	2	2
Salt and freshly ground black pepper			
Paprika			

method

1. Break the egg into a ramekin dish and prick the yolk with a cocktail stick (toothpick).

2. Soften the cream cheese on Medium for a few seconds then beat in the cream and lemon juice. Stir in the anchovies and season with salt and pepper.

3. Pour over the egg and sprinkle with paprika. Microwave on Low for 3-4 minutes until the egg is

just set. Leave to stand for a few minutes before serving.

 6-8 min Preparation time

QUICK OMELETTE

ingredients	Metric	Imperial	American
Butter or margarine	*15 ml*	*1 tsp*	*1 tsp*
Egg, separated	*1*	*1*	*1*
Milk	*15 ml*	*1 tbsp*	*1 tbsp*
Salt and freshly ground black pepper			

method

1. Place the butter in a dish and microwave on High for 30 seconds until melted.

2. Whisk the egg yolk, milk, salt and pepper. Beat the egg white until stiff. Fold the egg white into the yolk mixture.

3. Spoon into the dish and microwave on Low for 2-3 minutes until just set. Leave to stand for 1 minute before serving.

 6-7 min Preparation time

SAUSAGEMEAT SCRAMBLE

ingredients	Metric	Imperial	American
Sausagemeat	25 g	1 oz	2 tbsp
Eggs	2	2	2
Whipping (heavy) cream	15 ml	1 tbsp	1 tbsp
Grated Parmesan cheese	10 ml	2 tsp	2 tsp
Chopped fresh parsley	10 ml	2 tsp	2 tsp
Squeeze of lemon juice			
Pinch of dried basil			
Salt and freshly ground black pepper			
Mozzarella cheese, cubed	25 g	1 oz	2 tbsp
Button mushrooms, sliced	2	2	2
Black olives, sliced	3	3	3

method

1. Crumble the sausagemeat into a casserole, cover and microwave on High for 12 minutes until no longer pink. Drain.

2. Beat together the eggs, cream, Parmesan, parsley, lemon juice, basil, salt and pepper. Stir in the Mozzarella, mushrooms and olives. Pour over the sausagemeat.

3. Microwave on High for 2-4 minutes until the eggs are just set, stirring regularly during cooking.

4. Cover and leave to stand for 1 minute before serving.

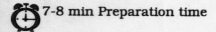 7-8 min Preparation time

42

PIPERADE

ingredients	Metric	Imperial	American
Canned chopped tomatoes, drained	100 g	4 oz	1/4 lb
Small green (bell) pepper, chopped	1	1	1
Shallot, chopped	1	1	1
Garlic clove, chopped	1/2	1/2	1/2
Oil	10 ml	2 tsp	2 tsp
Salt and freshly ground black pepper			
Pinch of dried oregano			
Few drops of tabasco sauce			
Eggs, beaten	2	2	2

method

1. Mix together the tomatoes, pepper, shallot, garlic and oil and microwave on High for 2-4 minutes until the peppers are soft. Season with salt, pepper, oregano and tabasco.

2. Pour the beaten eggs over the vegetable mixture and microwave on Medium for 2-3 minutes, stirring regularly, until the mixture is creamy. Serve with salad and buttered toast.

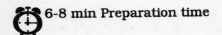 6-8 min Preparation time

MACARONI CHEESE

ingredients	Metric	Imperial	American
Macaroni	50 g	2 oz	½ cup
Boiling water	300 ml	½ pt	1¼ cups
Salt			
Butter or margarine	15 ml	1 tbsp	1 tbsp
Shallot, chopped	1	1	1
Lean bacon rasher (slice), rinded and chopped	1	1	1
Plain (all-purpose) flour	10 ml	2 tsp	2 tsp
Milk	150 ml	¼ pt	⅔ cup
Cheddar cheese, grated	50 g	2 oz	½ cup
Pinch of paprika			
Freshly ground black pepper			

method

1. Place the macaroni and boiling water in a bowl with a pinch of salt and microwave on High for 4-6 minutes, stirring twice during cooking. Drain.

2. Put the butter or margarine, shallot and bacon in a bowl and microwave on High for 2 minutes.

3. Stir in the flour then blend in the milk. Microwave on High for 2 minutes, stirring once during cooking.

4. Stir in the cheese and leave to stand for 1 minute.

5. Stir the macaroni into the sauce and season with paprika, salt and pepper. Microwave on High for 1-2 minutes until hot and well blended, stirring several times during cooking.

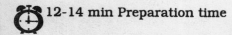 12-14 min Preparation time

44

CHEESE AND HAM TOASTIES

ingredients	Metric	Imperial	American
Bread slices, crusts removed	2	2	2
Wholegrain mustard	5 ml	1 tsp	1 tsp
Cheese, grated	50 g	2 oz	½ cup
Cooked ham slice	1	1	1
Butter or margarine			

method

1. Spread 1 slice of bread with mustard and top with cheese and ham. Sandwich with the other slice.

2. Melt the butter or margarine in a bowl on High for a few seconds.

3. Preheat a browning dish according to the manufacturer's instructions. Brush one side of the sandwich with butter and brown, butter side down, on High for about 45 seconds. Turn over, brush with butter and brown the underside for a further 50 seconds.

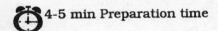 4-5 min Preparation time

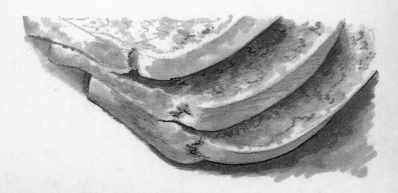

WELSH RAREBIT

ingredients	Metric	Imperial	American
Butter or margarine	15 ml	1 tbsp	1 tbsp
Cheese, grated	75 g	3 oz	¾ cup
Few drops of Worcestershire sauce			
Salt and freshly ground black pepper			
Double (heavy) cream	15 ml	1 tbsp	1 tbsp
Bread slice, toasted	1	1	1

method

1. Place the butter or margarine and cheese in a bowl and season with Worcestershire sauce, salt and pepper. Microwave on High for 1 minute until smooth. Stir well.

2. Stir in the cream and blend well. Microwave on High for 2-3 minutes, stirring regularly until smooth and thick.

3. Spread over the toast and serve at once.

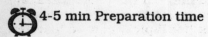 4-5 min Preparation time

BLUE CHEESE LOG

ingredients	Metric	Imperial	American
Butter or margarine	5 ml	1 tsp	1 tsp
Sesame seeds	15 ml	1 tbsp	1 tbsp
Cream cheese	100 g	4 oz	¼ lb
Blue cheese	25 g	1 oz	¼ cup
Sherry	5 ml	1 tsp	1 tsp
Few drops of Worcestershire sauce			
Pinch of crushed garlic			

method

1. Melt the butter in a dish on High for 20 seconds. Stir in the sesame seeds and microwave on High for about 1 minute until light brown, stirring once.

2. Put the cheeses in a dish and microwave on Medium for about 1 minute until they soften. Add the sherry, Worcestershire sauce and garlic and beat until light and fluffy. Chill for 1 hour until easy to handle.

3. Shape into a small log, roll in the toasted sesame seeds and microwave on Medium for 1-2 minutes until a cocktail stick (toothpick) can be inserted into the centre. Leave to stand for 5 minutes then serve with crackers.

9-12 min Preparation time plus chilling

Fish & Shellfish

COD WITH ONION-YOGHURT SAUCE

ingredients	Metric	Imperial	American
Cod fillets or steaks	100 g	4 oz	¼ lb
Milk or water	5 ml	1 tsp	1 tsp
Butter or margarine	5 ml	1 tsp	1 tsp
Salt and freshly ground black pepper			
Sauce:			
Butter or margarine	5 ml	1 tsp	1 tsp
Spring onion (scallion),sliced	1	1	1
Few drops of lemon juice			
Pinch of chopped fresh chives			
Pinch of chopped fresh parsley			
Mayonnaise	15 ml	1 tbsp	1 tbsp
Natural (plain) yoghurt	90 ml	6 tbsp	6 tbsp
Salt and freshly ground black pepper			

method

1. Arrange the fish in a shallow dish. If the fillets are thin or uneven, roll them up or fold them into thirds. If you are cooking fish steaks, arrange

them with the thickest portions to the outside of the dish. Spoon over the milk or water and dot with butter. Season lightly. Cover with a piece of damp kitchen paper.

2. Microwave on High for 2-3 minutes until the fish flakes easily when tested with a fork. Thicker fillets may take slightly longer.

3. To make the sauce, mix together the butter or margarine, spring onion, lemon juice and herbs in a small bowl and microwave on High for 1-2 minutes until the spring onion is tender but still crisp.

4. Leave to cool slightly, then stir in the mayonnaise and yoghurt and season to taste with salt and pepper.

🕐 10 min Preparation time

note

You can use any type of fish for this recipe.

49

COD IN CIDER SAUCE

ingredients	Metric	Imperial	American
Cod fillet	100 g	4 oz	¼ lb
Small onion, chopped	½	½	½
Button mushrooms, sliced	25 g	1 oz	½ cup
Butter or margarine	15 ml	1 tbsp	1 tbsp
Dry cider	75 ml	5 tbsp	5 tbsp
Salt and freshly ground black pepper			
Plain (all-purpose) flour	5 ml	1 tsp	1 tsp
Double (heavy) cream	15 ml	1 tbsp	1 tbsp
Chopped fresh parsley	5 ml	1 tsp	1 tsp

method

1. Skin the fish and place in a shallow dish. Arrange the onion and mushrooms over the fish and dot with the butter or margarine. Pour over the cider and season with salt and pepper. Microwave on High for 2-3 minutes until the fish flakes easily when tested with a fork.

2. Lift the fish out of the dish and place on a warm serving dish. Return the dish to the oven and microwave on High for 2-3 minutes. Stir in the flour and cream and microwave for 30 seconds. Whisk well until smooth. Stir in the parsley and pour over the fish.

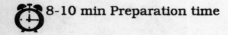 8-10 min Preparation time

COD IN CUCUMBER SAUCE

ingredients	Metric	Imperial	American
Water	15 ml	1 tbsp	1 tbsp
Lemon slice	1	1	1
Spring onion (scallion), sliced	1	1	1
Salt and freshly ground black pepper			
Bay leaf	½	½	½
Cod fillet	100 g	4 oz	¼ lb
Sauce:			
Spring onion (scallion), chopped	1	1	1
Soured (dairy sour) cream	45 ml	3 tbsp	3 tbsp
Cucumber, diced	5 cm	2 in	2 in
Milk	10 ml	2 tsp	2 tsp
Few drops of lemon juice			
Pinch of grated nutmeg			

method

1. Put the water, lemon, spring onion, salt, pepper and bayleaf in a dish, cover and microwave on High for 1-2 minutes. Stir well.

2. Arrange the fish in the dish, cover and microwave on High for 2-3 minutes until the fish flakes easily when tested with a fork. Transfer the fillets to a warm plate and set aside.

3. To make the sauce, place the spring onion in a bowl, cover and microwave on High for 30 seconds until soft.

4. Stir in the remaining ingredients and microwave on Medium for about 1 minute until hot. Stir well. Pour the sauce over the fish before serving.

 8-10 min Preparation time

COD IN ALMONDS AND OATMEAL

ingredients	Metric	Imperial	American
Ground almonds	25 g	1 oz	1/4 cup
Medium oatmeal	25 g	1 oz	1/4 cup
Chopped fresh parsley	5 ml	1 tsp	1 tsp
Pinch of paprika			
Salt and freshly ground black pepper			
Butter or margarine	5 ml	1 tsp	1 tsp
Egg	1/2	1/2	1/2
Cod fillet	100 g	4 oz	1/4 lb
Sauce:			
Butter or margarine	10 ml	2 tsp	2 tsp
Flaked almonds	15 ml	1 tbsp	1 tbsp

method

1. Mix the almonds, oatmeal, parsley, paprika, salt and pepper.

2. Put the butter or margarine in a dish and microwave on High for 20 seconds until melted. Blend in the egg. Dip the fish in the egg mixture then coat with the almond mixture.

3. Arrange the fish on a rack and cover with greaseproof (waxed) paper. Microwave on Medium for 3-5 minutes until the fish flakes easily when tested with a fork. Leave to stand for 1 minute.

4. Microwave the butter or margarine for the sauce on High for 20 seconds until melted. Stir in the flaked almonds. Microwave on High for 45 seconds until light brown. Spoon over the fish to serve.

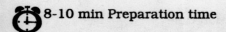 8-10 min Preparation time

FISH PIE

ingredients	Metric	Imperial	American
Butter or margarine	30 ml	2 tbsp	2 tbsp
Plain (all-purpose) flour	10 ml	2 tsp	2 tsp
Milk	75 ml	5 tbsp	5 tbsp
White fish, skinned	100 g	4 oz	¼ lb
Salt and freshly ground black pepper			
Mashed potato	25 g	1 oz	2 tbsp
Grated Cheddar cheese	15 ml	1 tbsp	1 tbsp
Tomato, sliced	1	1	1

method

1. Put half the butter or margarine in a jug and microwave on High for 15 seconds until melted. Stir in the flour then blend in the milk.

2. Microwave on High for 1-2 minutes until thick, stirring occasionally.

3. Place the fish on a plate, cover with microwave film and microwave on High for 2-3 minutes until cooked through. Flake the fish into a bowl, stir in the sauce.

4. Spoon the fish mixture into a suitable dish and season with salt and pepper. Mix the remaining butter or margarine into the mashed potato and pipe or spread the mashed potato evenly over the top and sprinkle with cheese. Microwave on High for 2-3 minutes until hot. Serve garnished with tomato.

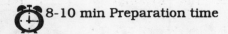 8-10 min Preparation time

FISH IN WINE SAUCE

ingredients	Metric	Imperial	American
Butter or margarine	10 ml	2 tsp	2 tsp
Plain (all-purpose) flour	10 ml	2 tsp	2 tsp
Salt and freshly ground black pepper			
Dry white wine	45 ml	3 tbsp	3 tbsp
Chicken stock	45 ml	3 tbsp	3 tbsp
Mushrooms, sliced	4	4	4
Peeled prawns (shrimp)	6	6	6
Cooked white fish, flaked	75 g	3 oz	6 tbsp
Chopped fresh parsley	10 ml	2 tsp	2 tsp

method

1. Melt the butter in a bowl on High for 30 seconds. Stir in the flour, salt and pepper then blend in the wine and stock. Microwave on High for 2-3 minutes until smooth, stirring once or twice during cooking.

2. Stir in the mushrooms, prawns and fish, cover and microwave on Medium for 3 minutes. Serve sprinkled with parsley.

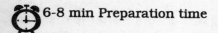 6-8 min Preparation time

FISH IN TOMATO-TABASCO SAUCE

ingredients	Metric	Imperial	American
Hot water	45 ml	3 tbsp	3 tbsp
Passata (sieved tomatoes)	45 ml	3 tbsp	3 tbsp
Shallot, chopped	1	1	1
Long-grain rice	15 ml	1 tbsp	1 tbsp
Pinch of dried basil			
Pinch of dried tarragon			
Few drops of tabasco sauce			
Salt			
Cod fillet, cubed	100 g	4 oz	¼ lb

method

1. Mix together all the ingredients except the fish and microwave on High for 2-3 minutes until hot and well blended.

2. Cover and microwave on Medium for about 5 minutes until the rice is just tender.

3. Stir in the cod, cover and microwave on Medium for 2-3 minutes until the fish flakes easily when tested with a fork. Leave to stand, covered, for 1 minute before serving.

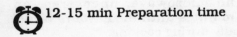 12-15 min Preparation time

SPICED TOMATO FISH

ingredients	Metric	Imperial	American
Red (bell) pepper, chopped	¼	¼	¼
Small celery stick, chopped	½	½	½
Spring onion (scallion), chopped	1	1	1
Olive oil	10 ml	2 tsp	2 tsp
Tomatoes	100 g	4 oz	¼ lb
Tomato purée (paste)	10 ml	2 tsp	2 tsp
Dry white wine	15 ml	1 tbsp	1 tbsp
Few drops of lemon juice			
Chopped fresh parsley	10 ml	2 tsp	2 tsp
Pinch of mustard powder			
Salt and freshly ground black pepper			
Cod or coley, cubed	100 g	4 oz	¼ lb

method

1. Put the pepper, celery, spring onion and oil into a casserole and microwave on High for 2-3 minutes until tender.

2. Stir in all the remaining ingredients except the fish, cover and microwave on High for 2-3 minutes. Stir well.

3. Add the fish and microwave, uncovered, on Medium for 5-8 minutes until the flavours blend, stirring occasionally during cooking.

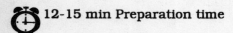 12-15 min Preparation time

FISH CURRY

ingredients	Metric	Imperial	American
Oil	10 ml	2 tsp	2 tsp
Spring onion (scallion), chopped	1	1	1
Cornflour (cornstarch)	5 ml	1 tsp	1 tsp
Curry powder	5 ml	1 tsp	1 tsp
Canned tomatoes, chopped	100 g	4 oz	¼ lb
Fish stock or water	75 ml	5 tbsp	5 tbsp
Few drops of lemon juice			
Salt and freshly ground black pepper			
Cod or haddock, cubed	100 g	4 oz	¼ lb

method

1. Place the oil and spring onion in a dish and microwave on High for 1-2 minutes until soft.

2. Stir in the cornflour then the remaining ingredients except the fish, seasoning to taste with curry powder, salt and pepper. Cover and microwave on High for 2-3 minutes, stirring once during cooking.

3. Add the fish and microwave on High for 1-2 minutes until the fish flakes easily when tested with a fork. Leave to stand for 5 minutes before serving.

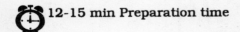 12-15 min Preparation time

HADDOCK WITH CHEESE

ingredients	Metric	Imperial	American
Haddock fillet	100 g	4 oz	¼ lb
Butter or margarine	15 ml	1 tbsp	1 tbsp
Capers, drained	15 ml	1 tbsp	1 tbsp
Parmesan cheese, grated	15 ml	1 tbsp	1 tbsp
Paprika			

method

1. Cut the haddock into large chunks and arrange in a casserole.

2. Put the butter or margarine in a bowl and microwave on High for 25 seconds until melted. Pour over the haddock. Sprinkle with the capers and microwave on High for 1-2 minutes.

3. Rearrange the fish, sprinkle with cheese and paprika and microwave on High for 2-3 minutes until the fish flakes easily when tested with a fork.

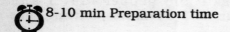 8-10 min Preparation time

KEDGEREE

ingredients	Metric	Imperial	American
Smoked haddock fillet	100 g	4 oz	¼ lb
Boiling water	150 ml	¼ pt	⅔ cup
Butter or margarine	15 ml	1 tbsp	1 tbsp
Spring onion (scallion), chopped	1	1	1
Long-grain rice	25 g	1 oz	2 tbsp
Salt and freshly ground black pepper			
Garnish:			
Hard-boiled (hard-cooked) egg, chopped	1	1	1
Chopped fresh parsley	10 ml	2 tsp	2 tsp
Butter or margarine	15 ml	1 tbsp	1 tbsp

method

1. Put the haddock in a shallow dish and cover with boiling water. Microwave on High for 2 minutes. Drain, reserving the cooking liquid. Remove the skin from the fish and flake the flesh.

2. Put the butter or margarine in a casserole dish and microwave on High for 20 seconds. Add the spring onion and microwave for 30 seconds. Add the rice and pour over the fish cooking liquid. Microwave on High for 5-7 minutes until the liquid has been absorbed.

3. Stir in the fish and season to taste. Stir in the garnish ingredients and microwave on High for 30 seconds until heated through. Serve at once.

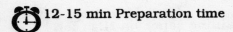 12-15 min Preparation time

SALMON AND PRAWN KEBABS

ingredients	Metric	Imperial	American
Small salmon steak	1	1	1
Peeled king prawns (shrimp)	50 g	2 oz	½ cup
Small white onions	2	2	2
Red (bell) pepper, cut			
into chunks	¼	¼	¼
Lemon, sliced	¼	¼	¼
Butter or margarine	10 ml	2 tsp	2 tsp
Sauce:			
Butter or margarine	25 g	1 oz	2 tbsp
Dry white wine	15 ml	1 tbsp	1 tbsp
Chopped fresh parsley	10 ml	2 tsp	2 tsp
Pepper			

method

1. Remove any bones from the salmon and cut into cubes. Thread the salmon, prawns, onions, pepper and lemon alternately on 2 wooden skewers.

2. Put the butter or margarine in a small bowl and microwave on High for a few seconds until melted. Brush over the seafood.

3. Put the butter or margarine for the sauce in a bowl and microwave on High for 20 seconds until melted. Beat in the remaining ingredients.

4. Place the kebabs on a roasting rack and brush with the sauce. Microwave on High for 2 minutes. Brush again with the sauce and microwave on High for 2-3 minutes until the fish flakes easily when tested with a fork.

5. Reheat the remaining sauce on High for 15-20 seconds and serve separately.

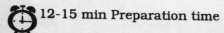 12-15 min Preparation time

MINTED SALMON CUTLET

ingredients	Metric	Imperial	American
Red wine vinegar	10 ml	2 tsp	2 tsp
Olive oil	10 ml	2 tsp	2 tsp
Few drops of honey			
Chopped fresh mint	15 ml	1 tbsp	1 tbsp
Salmon cutlet	1	1	1

method

1. Mix together the wine vinegar, oil, honey and mint. Microwave on High for about 30 seconds until just boiling, stirring once during cooking.

2. Place the salmon into the dressing and turn to coat with the mixture. Cover and chill for 1 hour, turning once.

3. Turn the salmon again, cover and microwave on Medium for 3-4 minutes until the fish flakes when tested with a fork. Drain and serve hot or cold.

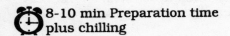
8-10 min Preparation time
plus chilling

SALMON WITH DILL SAUCE

ingredients	Metric	Imperial	American
Salmon steak	1	1	1
Sauce:			
Butter or margarine	10 ml	2 tsp	2 tsp
Lemon juice	10 ml	2 tsp	2 tsp
Pinch of sugar			
Chopped fresh dill	2.5 ml	½ tsp	½ tsp
Salt and freshly ground black pepper			
Shallot, finely chopped	½	½	½

method

1. Put all the sauce ingredients in a bowl and microwave on High for 30 seconds until the mixture is hot. Stir well.

2. Put the steak on a roasting rack and brush with the sauce. Cover with grease proof (waxed) paper and microwave on Medium for 5-8 minutes until the fish flakes easily when tested with a fork. Leave to stand for 2-3 minutes.

3. Microwave the remaining sauce on High for about 30 seconds and serve separately.

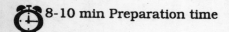 8-10 min Preparation time

SALMON IN RED WINE

ingredients	Metric	Imperial	American
Salmon steak	1	1	1
Sauce:			
Butter or margarine	10 ml	2 tsp	2 tsp
Red wine	15 ml	1 tbsp	1 tbsp
Pinch of dried chervil			
Pinch of celery salt			
Pinch of paprika			
Salt and freshly ground black pepper			

method

1. Mix together the sauce ingredients and microwave on High for about 1 minute until the butter melts.

2. Place the salmon in a dish and brush over half the sauce. Cover with greaseproof (waxed) paper and microwave on Medium for 6-7 minutes until the fish flakes easily when tested with a fork, basting occasionally with the remaining sauce.

3. Cover and leave to stand for 2 minutes before serving.

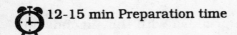 12-15 min Preparation time

TROUT WITH TOASTED ALMONDS

ingredients	Metric	Imperial	American
Trout, cleaned	1	1	1
Few drops of lemon juice			
Salt and freshly ground black pepper			
Butter or margarine	15 ml	1 tbsp	1 tbsp
Flaked almonds	30 ml	2 tbsp	2 tbsp
A few fresh parsley sprigs			
Lemon slices	2	2	2

method

1. Lay the fish in an oval dish, sprinkle with lemon juice and season with salt and pepper. Cover with microwave film and microwave on High for 4-5 minutes. Leave to stand, covered, while you prepare the almonds.

2. Place the butter or margarine and almonds in a small bowl and microwave on High for 1-2 minutes, stirring frequently until the almonds are lightly browned.

3. Serve the trout sprinkled with the almonds and garnish with parsley and lemon slices.

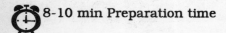 8-10 min Preparation time

STUFFED TROUT

ingredients	Metric	Imperial	American
Celery stick, chopped	½	½	½
Spring onion (scallion), chopped	½	½	½
Butter or margarine	15 ml	1 tbsp	1 tbsp
Button mushrooms, sliced	25 g	1 oz	½ cup
Chopped fresh parsley	15 ml	1 tbsp	1 tbsp
Grated lemon rind	2.5 ml	½ tsp	½ tsp
Pinch of dried dill			
Salt and freshly ground black pepper			
Breadcrumbs	25 ml	1½ tbsp	1½ tbsp
Peeled prawns (shrimp), chopped	50 g	2 oz	½ cup
Trout, gutted	1	1	1

method

1. Put the celery, spring onion and butter or margarine in a bowl and microwave on High for 2-3 minutes until the celery is tender.

2. Stir in the mushrooms, parsley, lemon rind, dill, salt, pepper and breadcrumbs. Stir in the prawns. Spoon the stuffing into the trout.

3. Place the trout on a roasting rack and cover with greaseproof (waxed) paper. Microwave on Medium for 6-8 minutes until the fish flakes easily when tested with a fork, rearranging several times during cooking.

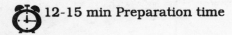 12-15 min Preparation time

BAKED CRAB

ingredients	Metric	Imperial	American
Butter or margarine	10 ml	2 tsp	2 tsp
Spring onion (scallion), chopped	1	1	1
Dry sherry	10 ml	2 tsp	2 tsp
Crab meat	50 g	2 oz	1/8 lb
Breadcrumbs	15 ml	1 tbsp	1 tbsp
Pinch of made mustard			
Few drops of Worcestershire sauce			
Chopped fresh parsley	10 ml	2 tsp	2 tsp
Salt and freshly ground black pepper			
Browned breadcrumbs	15 ml	1 tbsp	1 tbsp
Grated Gruyère cheese	10 ml	2 tsp	2 tsp

method

1. Put the butter or margarine and spring onion in a shallow dish and microwave on High for 20 seconds.

2. Stir in the sherry, crab meat, breadcrumbs, mustard, Worcestershire sauce, parsley, salt and pepper. Microwave on High for 1 minute.

3. Mix together the browned breadcrumbs and Gruyère and sprinkle over the dish. Microwave on High for about 1 minute until the cheese has melted. Serve at once.

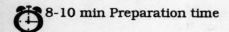 8-10 min Preparation time

PRAWN PILAU

ingredients	Metric	Imperial	American
Small onion, sliced	1	1	1
Small green chilli, seeded and chopped	1	1	1
Garlic clove, crushed	1/2	1/2	1/2
Bacon rasher (slice), rinded and chopped	1	1	1
Long-grain rice	25 g	1 oz	2 tbsp
Canned tomatoes	100 g	4 oz	1/4 lb
Salt and freshly ground black pepper			
Chicken stock	120 ml	4 fl oz	1/2 cup
Peeled prawns (shrimp)	100 g	4 oz	1 cup
Chopped fresh parsley	10 ml	2 tsp	2 tsp

method

1. Put the onion, chilli, garlic and bacon in a casserole dish and microwave on High for 2-3 minutes until soft.

2. Add the rice, tomatoes and their juice, salt, pepper and stock, cover and microwave on Medium for 3-4 minutes, stirring once.

3. Stir in the prawns and microwave on High for 1½ minutes. Leave to stand for 2 minutes then serve sprinkled with parsley.

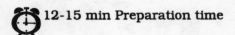 12-15 min Preparation time

SPICY PRAWNS

ingredients	Metric	Imperial	American
Spring onion (scallion), chopped	1	1	1
Grated ginger root	5 ml	1 tsp	1 tsp
Tomato purée (paste)	15 ml	1 tbsp	1 tbsp
Few drops of tabasco sauce			
Few drops of soy sauce			
Dry sherry	10 ml	2 tsp	2 tsp
Peeled prawns (shrimp)	100 g	4 oz	1 cup

method

1. Mix the spring onion, ginger, tomato purée, tabasco and soy sauces and sherry. Microwave on High for 1 minute until hot.

2. Stir in the prawns until well coated. Microwave on High for 1-2 minutes until heated through.

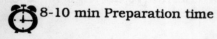 8-10 min Preparation time

Poultry

CHICKEN AND BROCCOLI LAYER

ingredients	Metric	Imperial	American
Slices wholewheat bread	2-3	2-3	2-3
Cooked or frozen broccoli, chopped	50 g	2 oz	1/8 lb
Cooked chicken, cubed	100 g	4 oz	1/4 lb
Gruyère cheese, grated	50 g	2 oz	1/2 cup
Milk	75 ml	5 tbsp	5 tbsp
Small egg, beaten	1	1	1
Pinch of mustard powder			
Pinch of cayenne pepper			

method

1. Use the bread slices to line an individual pie plate. Top with broccoli, chicken and half the cheese.

2. Blend together the milk, egg, mustard and cayenne. Pour over the broccoli mixture, cover and refrigerate until cold, or overnight if possible.

3. Microwave on High for 2 minutes then on Medium for 6-8 minutes until a knife inserted in the centre comes out clean. Sprinkle with the remaining cheese. Leave to stand for 2 minutes before serving.

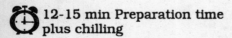 12-15 min Preparation time
plus chilling

GOLDEN CRUNCHY CHICKEN

ingredients	Metric	Imperial	American
Boneless chicken breast	1	1	1
Cheddar cheese slice	1	1	1
Butter or margarine	15 ml	1 tbsp	1 tbsp
Fried bread slice, crushed	1	1	1
Salt and freshly ground black pepper			

method

1. Place the chicken on a baking dish, cover with greaseproof (waxed) paper and microwave on High for 4-5 minutes until cooked through, rearranging once or twice during cooking.

2. Place the cheese on the top and microwave on High for 30 seconds until softened.

3. Mix together the butter or margarine, breadcrumbs, salt and pepper. Sprinkle the mixture over the chicken and press lightly into the cheese. Microwave on High for 30-60 seconds.

 8-10 min Preparation time

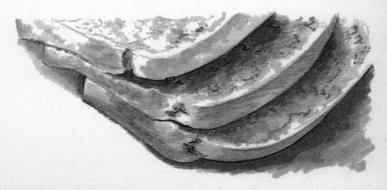

ORANGE CHICKEN

ingredients	Metric	Imperial	American
Chicken portion	1	1	1
Unsweetened orange juice	75 ml	5 tbsp	5 tbsp
Small garlic clove, crushed	½	½	½
Pinch of paprika			
Chopped fresh parsley	5 ml	1 tsp	1 tsp
Orange slices	3	3	3

method

1. Place the chicken portion in a baking dish, pour over the orange juice and sprinkle with garlic. Cover and microwave on High for 8-10 minutes, turning several times during cooking and basting with the orange juice.

2. Sprinkle with paprika, cover and microwave on High for 1½ minutes until the chicken is thoroughly cooked. Cover and leave to stand for 2 minutes.

3. Serve garnished with parsley and orange slices.

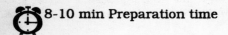 8-10 min Preparation time

CHICKEN WITH TOMATOES

ingredients	Metric	Imperial	American
Mushrooms, sliced	25 g	1 oz	½ cup
Small onion, sliced	1	1	1
Olive oil	10 ml	2 tsp	2 tsp
Garlic cloves, crushed	½	½	½
Canned tomatoes	100 g	4 oz	¼ lb
Tomato purée	10 ml	2 tsp	2 tsp
Dry white wine	15 ml	1 tbsp	1 tbsp
Bay leaf	½	½	½
Pinch of dried basil			
Salt and freshly ground black pepper			
Boneless chicken breast, skinned and cubed	1	1	1

method

1. Put the mushrooms, onion, oil and garlic into a casserole, cover and microwave on High for 2-3 minutes until soft, stirring once.

2. Stir in the remaining ingredients, cover and microwave on High for 5-6 minutes until the chicken is cooked through, stirring once or twice during cooking.

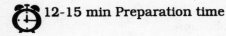 12-15 min Preparation time

BREADED CHICKEN STRIPS

ingredients	Metric	Imperial	American
Natural (plain) yoghurt	60 ml	4 tbsp	4 tbsp
Chopped onion	5 ml	1 tsp	1 tsp
Garlic clove, crushed	½	½	½
Pinch of crushed fennel seed			
Boneless chicken breast	1	1	1
Dry breadcrumbs	60 ml	4 tbsp	4 tbsp
Grated Parmesan cheese	10 ml	2 tsp	2 tsp
Pinch of paprika			

method

1. Mix the yoghurt, onion, garlic and fennel.

2. Remove the chicken skin and cut the flesh into strips. Stir into the yoghurt mixture and leave to marinate, if possible, for 2 hours.

3. Mix the breadcrumbs, Parmesan and paprika. Roll the chicken strips in the mixture, pressing lightly to coat.

4. Arrange the chicken on a roasting rack and microwave on Medium for 3-5 minutes until the chicken is firm and no longer pink, rearranging once during cooking.

8-10 min Preparation time
plus marinating

CHICKEN WITH RICE

ingredients	Metric	Imperial	American
Butter or margarine	15 ml	1 tbsp	1 tbsp
Small shallot, chopped	1	1	1
Plain (all-purpose) flour	15 ml	1 tbsp	1 tbsp
Chicken stock	60 ml	4 tbsp	4 tbsp
Milk	45 ml	3 tbsp	3 tbsp
Pinch of cayenne			
Salt and freshly ground black pepper			
Cooked chicken, diced	50 g	2 oz	4 tbsp
Cooked ham, diced	15 g	1 oz	2 tbsp
Cooked long-grain rice	50 g	2 oz	4 tbsp

method

1. Put the butter or margarine and shallot in a
    shallow dish and microwave on High for 20
    seconds. Stir in the flour then blend in the stock,
    milk, cayenne, salt and pepper. Microwave on
    High for 1 minute until thick, stirring at least once
    during cooking.

2. Add the chicken and ham, cover and microwave on
    High for 3-4 minutes, stirring once or twice during
    cooking.

3. Remove the cover and spoon the rice around the
    dish. Microwave on High for 1-2 minutes until the
    rice is hot.

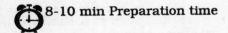 8-10 min Preparation time

STUFFED CHICKEN WITH MUSHROOM SAUCE

ingredients	Metric	Imperial	American
Butter or margarine	10 ml	2 tsp	2 tsp
Mushrooms, chopped	50 g	2 oz	½ cup
Chopped onion	10 ml	2 tsp	2 tsp
Chopped celery	10 ml	2 tsp	2 tsp
Garlic clove, crushed	½	½	½
Dried breadcrumbs	45 ml	3 tbsp	3 tbsp
Salt and freshly ground black pepper			
Boneless chicken breast, skinned	1	1	1
Egg, beaten	1	1	1
Sauce:			
Butter or margarine	15 ml	1 tbsp	1 tbsp
Mushrooms, sliced	50 g	2 oz	½ cup
Plain (all-purpose) flour	15 ml	1 tbsp	1 tbsp
Dry white wine	45 ml	3 tbsp	3 tbsp
Milk or single (light) cream	150 ml	¼ pt	⅔ cup
Salt and freshly ground black pepper			

method

1. Place the butter or margarine, mushrooms, onion, celery and garlic in a bowl and microwave on High for 1-2 minutes until soft. Stir in 15 ml/1 tbsp of the breadcrumbs and season with salt and pepper.

2. Place the chicken breast between two sheets of microwave film or greaseproof (waxed) paper and pound to flatten them. Spoon the stuffing mixture on top, fold the chicken to surround it and secure with cocktail sticks (toothpicks).

3. Dip the chicken breasts in egg and sprinkle with the remaining breadcrumbs. Place in a baking

dish and cover with greaseproof (waxed) paper. Microwave on Medium for 5-7 minutes until the chicken is cooked through, checking once or twice during cooking.

4. To make the sauce, place the butter or margarine and mushrooms in a bowl and microwave on High for 1-2 minutes until soft. Stir in the flour then blend in the wine and milk or cream. Season with salt and pepper. Microwave on High for 1-2 minutes until thick, stirring twice during cooking.

 12-15 min Preparation time

COQ AU VIN

ingredients	Metric	Imperial	American
Spring onion (scallion), sliced	1	1	1
Small garlic clove, crushed	½	½	½
Bacon rasher (slice), rinded and chopped	1	1	1
Plain (all-purpose) flour	10 ml	2 tsp	2 tsp
Hot water	45 ml	3 tbsp	3 tbsp
Red wine	15 ml	1 tbsp	1 tbsp
Chicken portion, skinned	1	1	1
Button mushrooms, sliced	50 g	2 oz	½ cup
Chopped fresh parsley	5 ml	1 tsp	1 tsp
Pinch of dried tarragon			
Salt and freshly ground black pepper			
To serve:			
Red wine	15 ml	1 tbsp	1 tbsp

method

1. Place the spring onion and garlic in a bowl, cover and microwave on High for 1 minute until soft. Set aside.

2. Put the bacon in a casserole and microwave on High for 2-3 minutes until crisp, stirring once. Drain, reserving 5 ml/1 tsp of fat in the casserole. Crumble the bacon and set aside.

3. Stir the flour into the casserole with the water and wine. Add the chicken pieces and the remaining ingredients except the serving wine. Cover and microwave on High for 8-10 minutes until the chicken is cooked through, rearranging the chicken once and stirring occasionally during cooking. Stir in the remaining wine and serve hot.

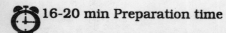 16-20 min Preparation time

CHICKEN CURRY

ingredients	Metric	Imperial	American
Oil	5 ml	1 tsp	1 tsp
Spring onion (scallion), sliced	1	1	1
Green (bell) pepper, diced	¼	¼	¼
Garlic clove, crushed	1	1	1
Curry powder	5 ml	1 tsp	1 tsp
Ground allspice	2.5 ml	½ tsp	½ tsp
Pinch of ground ginger			
Salt and freshly ground black pepper			
Chicken portion	1	1	1
Tomato, skinned and chopped	1	1	1
Chicken stock	75 ml	5 tbsp	5 tbsp
Dessert apple, peeled, cored and sliced	¼	¼	¼

method

1. Put the oil, spring onion, pepper and garlic in a casserole and microwave on High for 2-3 minutes.

2. Mix together the curry powder, all-spice, ginger, salt and pepper and rub over the chicken. Add to the casserole with the tomatoes and stock, cover and microwave on High for 6-8 minutes. Stir well.

3. Add the apple, cover and microwave on High for 4-5 minutes until the chicken is cooked through and tender. Serve with rice and chutney.

 16-20 min Preparation time

CHICKEN WITH MUSHROOM SAUCE

ingredients	Metric	Imperial	American
Spring onion (scallion), chopped	1	1	1
Butter or margarine	15 ml	1 tbsp	1 tbsp
Chicken portion	1	1	1
Button mushrooms, sliced	50 g	2 oz	½ cup
Milk	150 ml	¼ pt	⅔ cup
Cornflour (cornstarch)	10 ml	2 tsp	2 tsp
Salt and freshly ground black pepper			

method

1. Place the spring onion and half the butter or margarine in a casserole and microwave on High for 1 minute.

2. Add the chicken, cover and microwave on High for 8-10 minutes until cooked through. Drain off the cooking juices.

3. Put the remaining butter or margarine in a bowl and microwave on High for 20 seconds. Add the mushrooms, cover and microwave on High for 45 seconds.

4. Mix the cornflour with a little of the milk. Add the remaining milk to the mushrooms with the chicken cooking liquid. Microwave on High for 1-1½ minutes. Stir in the cornflour mixture, salt and pepper and microwave on High for 2 minutes, stirring occasionally until thickened.

5. Arrange the chicken on a warm serving plate, pour over the sauce and serve at once.

 16-20 min Preparation time

CUMIN CHICKEN

ingredients	Metric	Imperial	American
White wine vinegar	5 ml	2 tsp	2 tsp
Pinch of garlic salt			
Pinch of ground cumin			
Pinch of dried oregano			
Pinch of allspice			
Pinch of ground cloves			
Salt and freshly ground black pepper			
Chicken portion	1	1	1

method

1. Put all the ingredients except the chicken into a small bowl and mix thoroughly. Brush over the chicken.

2. Place the chicken on a roasting rack, cover with greaseproof (waxed) paper and microwave on High for 5-8 minutes until the juices run clear, turning twice during cooking.

3. Cover and leave to stand for 2 minutes before serving.

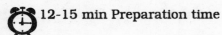 12-15 min Preparation time

CREAMY CHICKEN SUPREME

ingredients	Metric	Imperial	American
Butter or margarine	5 ml	1 tsp	1 tsp
Shallot, chopped	1	1	1
Plain (all-purpose) flour	5 ml	1 tsp	1 tsp
Chicken breast, cubed	100 g	4 oz	1/4 lb
Milk	75 ml	5 tbsp	5 tbsp
Chicken stock	75 ml	5 tbsp	5 tbsp
Salt and freshly ground black pepper			

method

1. Place the butter or margarine and shallot in a dish and microwave on High for 30 seconds until melted.

2. Stir in the flour and microwave on High for 30 seconds. Stir well.

3. Add the chicken then blend in the milk and stock and season with salt and pepper. Cover and microwave on High for 3-4 minutes until the chicken is cooked through and the sauce is smooth and thickened.

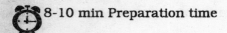 8-10 min Preparation time

CHINESE CHICKEN

ingredients	Metric	Imperial	American
Egg white	½	½	½
Cornflour (cornstarch)	7.5 ml	½ tbsp	½ tbsp
Pinch of sugar			
Chicken, cubed			
Oil	10 ml	2 tsp	2 tsp
Salted cashew nuts	25 g	1 oz	¼ cup
Pinch of ground ginger			
Soy sauce	5 ml	1 tsp	1 tsp
Dry sherry	5 ml	1 tsp	1 tsp
Garlic clove, crushed	½	½	½

method

1. Beat the egg white lightly then mix in the cornflour and sugar. Stir in the chicken pieces and leave in the refrigerator for 30 minutes.

2. Put a little oil in a shallow dish. Lift the chicken from the egg white with a slotted spoon and microwave on High for 1-2 minutes.

3. Put the remaining oil and the nuts in a separate bowl and microwave on High for 50 seconds. Stir in the ginger, soy sauce, sherry and garlic. Stir in the chicken and microwave on High for 45 seconds until the chicken is tender and the ingredients are well blended. Serve with rice and bean sprouts.

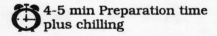 4-5 min Preparation time
plus chilling

CHICKEN AND MANGETOUT

ingredients	Metric	Imperial	American
Cornflour (cornstarch)	10 ml	2 tsp	2 tsp
Soy sauce	30 ml	2 tbsp	2 tbsp
Grated ginger root	5 ml	1 tsp	1 tsp
Boneless chicken breast, skinned and cut into strips	1	1	1
Mangetout (snow peas)	100 g	4 oz	¼ lb
Cashew nuts	50 g	2 oz	½ cup

method

1. Mix together the cornflour, soy sauce and ginger in a bowl. Microwave on High for 1 minute.

2. Add the chicken and stir until well coated in the mixture. Cover and microwave on High for about 3 minutes.

3. Stir in the mangetout, cover and microwave on High for 2-4 minutes until the chicken is cooked through, stirring twice during cooking.

4. Stir in the cashew nuts and serve with rice or noodles.

 12-15 min Preparation time

CARIBBEAN CHICKEN

ingredients	Metric	Imperial	American
Canned pineapple chunks in juice	50 g	2 oz	1/3 cup
Cornflour (cornstarch)	5 ml	1 tsp	1 tsp
Pinch of mustard powder			
Pinch of ground ginger			
Soy sauce	10 ml	2 tsp	2 tsp
Tomato ketchup (catsup)	10 ml	2 tsp	2 tsp
Boneless chicken breast, cubed	100 g	4 oz	1/4 lb
Small courgette (zucchini), sliced	1	1	1
Small carrot, chopped	1	1	1
Spring onion (scallion), chopped	1	1	1

method

1. Drain the pineapple chunks and reserve 45 ml/3 tbsp of juice. Blend the juice with the cornflour, mustard, ginger, soy sauce and ketchup. Stir in the chicken, courgette and carrot, cover and microwave on High for 5-6 minutes until the sauce is thick and the meat is tender, stirring twice during cooking.

2. Stir in the spring onion and pineapple chunks, cover and microwave on High for about 1 minute until heated through. Serve hot with rice.

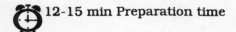 12-15 min Preparation time

85

SWEET AND SOUR TURKEY

ingredients	Metric	Imperial	American
Turkey cutlet	100 g	4 oz	¼ lb
Grated carrot	15 ml	1 tbsp	1 tbsp
Marinade:			
Orange juice	15 ml	1 tbsp	1 tbsp
Soft brown sugar	5 ml	1 tsp	1 tsp
Wine vinegar	2.5 ml	½ tsp	½ tsp
Pinch of ground ginger			
Salt			
Glaze:			
Orange marmalade	15 ml	1 tbsp	1 tbsp
Dijon mustard	1.5 ml	¼ tsp	¼ tsp

method

1. Cut the turkey into thin strips. Mix together the
    marinade ingredients and microwave on High for
    20 seconds until hot. Stir in the turkey strips and
    leave to marinate for up to 4 hours.

2. Remove the turkey from the marinade and mix
    with the carrot. Mix together the glaze ingredients
    and stir in 5 ml/1 tsp of the marinade. Toss the
    turkey and carrot in the glaze and microwave on
    High for 4-5 minutes until the turkey is cooked
    through.

8-10 min Preparation time
plus marinating

TURKEY WITH APRICOTS

ingredients	Metric	Imperial	American
Canned apricot halves in syrup	100 g	4 oz	$\frac{1}{4}$ lb
Turkey breast portion	1	1	1
Spring onions (scallions), sliced	2	2	2
Cornflour (cornstarch)	5 ml	1 tsp	1 tsp
French mustard			

method

1. Drain the apricots and reserve the syrup.

2. Place the turkey in a dish and sprinkle with the apricot halves and spring onions. Blend the cornflour into 75 ml/5 tbsp of the reserved syrup, blend in a little mustard to taste and pour over the turkey.

3. Cover and microwave on Medium for 5-8 minutes until the turkey is no longer pink and the sauce has thickened, stirring several times during cooking.

4. Slice the turkey across the grain and spoon the sauce over to serve.

12-15 min Preparation time

DUCK WITH CHERRY SAUCE

ingredients	Metric	Imperial	American
Canned cherries	100 g	4 oz	¼ lb
Cornflour (cornstarch)	2.5 ml	½ tsp	½ tsp
Red wine	15 ml	1 tbsp	1 tbsp
Honey	10 ml	2 tsp	2 tsp
Pinch of mustard powder			
Pinch of ground ginger			
Duck portion	1	1	1

method

1. Blend the cornflour with a little of the cherry juice then stir in the wine, honey, mustard and ginger and microwave for 30-60 seconds until thickened. Stir in the cherries and set aside.

2. Place the duck on a rack and microwave on Medium for 12-16 minutes per 450 g/1 lb until the juices run clear, turning over and draining the fat and basting with a little of the sauce once or twice during cooking. If necessary, shield bones or narrower portions with small pieces of foil.

3. Spoon the sauce over the duck and leave to stand for 2 minutes before serving.

 16-20 min Preparation time

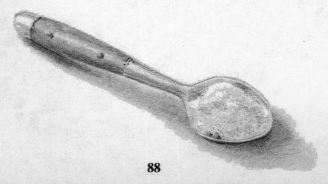

MEAT

BURGUNDY BEEF

ingredients	Metric	Imperial	American
Egg noodles	100 g	4 oz	¼ lb
Oil	5 ml	1 tsp	1 tsp
Minced (ground) beef	100 g	4 oz	¼ lb
Garlic clove, crushed	½	½	½
Button onions	4	4	4
Carrot, sliced	1	1	1
Mushrooms, sliced	50 g	2 oz	½ cup
Pinch of dried thyme			
Chopped fresh parsley	15 ml	1 tbsp	1 tbsp
Salt and freshly ground black pepper			
Beef stock or water	45 ml	3 tbsp	3 tbsp
Dry red wine	30 ml	2 tbsp	2 tbsp

method

1. Cook the noodles in boiling water as directed on the packet. Drain well.

2. Meanwhile, mix together the oil, beef, garlic and onions, cover and microwave on High for 2-4

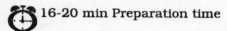

minutes until the meat is no longer pink, stirring once or twice during cooking.

3. Stir in the carrot, mushrooms, thyme, 5 ml/1 tsp of the parsley and the drained noodles and season with salt and pepper. Mix in the stock and wine.

4. Cover and microwave on High for 5-10 minutes until cooked through and well blended, stirring once or twice during cooking. Serve sprinkled with the remaining parsley.

16-20 min Preparation time

QUICK GOULASH

ingredients	Metric	Imperial	American
Butter or margarine	15 ml	1 tbsp	1 tbsp
Chuck steak, cubed	100 g	4 oz	¼ lb
Small onion, chopped	1	1	1
Garlic clove, crushed	½	½	½
Paprika	2.5 ml	½ tsp	½ tsp
Pinch of sugar			
Pinch of caraway seeds			
Canned tomatoes, chopped	50 g	2 oz	¼ cup
Soured (dairy sour) cream	10 ml	2 tsp	2 tsp
Salt and freshly ground black pepper			

method

1. Melt the butter on High for 20 seconds. Add the steak, onion and garlic and stir well. Cover and microwave on Medium for 8-9 minutes, stirring once or twice.

2. Add the paprika, sugar, caraway seeds and tomatoes and stir well. cover and microwave on Medium for 8 minutes until the meat is tender.

3. Stir in the soured cream and season to taste. Cover and leave to stand for 2-3 minutes before serving.

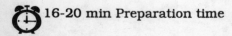 16-20 min Preparation time

PEPPER STEAK

ingredients	Metric	Imperial	American
Rump steak	175 g	6 oz	³/₈ cup
Shallot, sliced	1	1	1
Garlic clove, crushed	½	½	½
Beef stock	30 ml	2 tbsp	2 tbsp
Soy sauce	10 ml	2 tsp	2 tsp
Cornflour (cornstarch)	5 ml	1 tsp	1 tsp
Pinch of sugar			
Small green or red (bell) pepper, cut into chunks	1	1	1

method

1. Beat the steak until 5 mm/¼ in thick. Arrange in a casserole and sprinkle with the shallot and garlic. Mix together the stock, soy sauce, cornflour and sugar and pour over the steak. Cover and microwave on High for 2 minutes. Microwave on Medium for about 10 minutes until the beef is almost cooked to your liking, turning the pieces once or twice during cooking.

2. Add the pepper and microwave on Medium for 4-5 minutes until the peppers are softened but still crisp. Serve with rice.

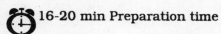 16-20 min Preparation time

MEXICAN BEEF

ingredients	Metric	Imperial	American
Minced (ground) beef	225 g	8 oz	½ lb
Shallot, chopped	1	1	1
Chilli powder	1.5 ml	¼ tsp	¼ tsp
Salt and freshly ground black pepper			
Pinch of ground cumin			
Pinch of dried oregano			
Garlic clove, chopped	1	1	1
Garnish:			
Tomato, sliced	1	1	1
Shallot, sliced	1	1	1

method

1. Mix the beef and shallot in a casserole and microwave on High for 2-3 minutes until no longer pink, stirring once or twice during cooking.

2. Stir in the remaining ingredients, cover and microwave on Medium for 2-3 minutes until the flavours blend, stirring once or twice. Garnish with tomato and onion and serve with tacos.

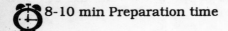 8-10 min Preparation time

SAVOURY MINCE

ingredients	Metric	Imperial	American
Small shallot, sliced	1	1	1
Carrot, sliced	1	1	1
Celery stick, sliced	½	½	½
Butter or margarine	15 ml	1 tbsp	1 tbsp
Minced (ground) beef	100 g	4 oz	¼ lb
Canned chopped tomatoes	100 g	4 oz	¼ lb
Salt and freshly ground black pepper			
Cornflour (cornstarch)	5 ml	1 tsp	1 tsp

method

1. Mix the shallot, carrot, celery and butter or margarine in a casserole and microwave on High for about 2 minutes until soft.

2. Stir in the beef and tomatoes and season with salt and pepper. Blend the cornflour with a little water and stir it into the beef. Cover and microwave on Medium for 6-8 minutes until cooked through and well blended. Adjust the seasoning before serving.

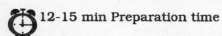 12-15 min Preparation time

VEAL WITH MARSALA SAUCE

ingredients	Metric	Imperial	American
Mushrooms, sliced	25 g	1 oz	½ cup
Chicken stock	90 ml	6 tbsp	6 tbsp
Marsala wine	30 ml	2 tbsp	2 tbsp
Chopped fresh parsley	5 ml	1 tsp	1 tsp
Salt and freshly ground black pepper			
Veal steak, 1 cm/½ in thick	100 g	4 oz	¼ lb
Plain (all-purpose) flour	5 ml	1 tsp	1 tsp
Milk	10 ml	2 tsp	2 tsp

method

1. Mix the mushrooms, stock, wine, parsley, salt and pepper in a baking dish. Cover with microwave film and microwave on High for 1-2 minutes until the mushrooms are tender, stirring once during cooking.

2. Add the veal and turn to coat in the mixture. Cover and microwave on Medium for 3-4 minutes until the veal is almost cooked. Remove the veal from the dish.

3. Blend the flour and milk together and stir into the stock. Microwave on High for 2-3 minutes until the sauce thickens and bubbles, stirring regularly. Pour over the veal to serve.

 12-15 min Preparation time

GINGERED LAMB CHOP

ingredients	Metric	Imperial	American
Butter or margarine	15 ml	1 tbsp	1 tbsp
Few drops of lemon juice			
Grated lemon rind	2.5 ml	½ tsp	½ tsp
Pinch of ground ginger			
Pinch of crushed garlic			
Salt and freshly ground black pepper			
Lamb chump chop	1	1	1

method

1. Place the butter or margarine in a small bowl and microwave on High for 20 seconds until melted. Stir in all the remaining ingredients except the chop.

2. Place the chop in a shallow dish. Brush with the seasoned butter on both sides. Microwave on High for 3-5 minutes until cooked, turning the chop once or twice during cooking.

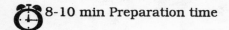 8-10 min Preparation time

LAMB CHOPS WITH LEMON

ingredients	Metric	Imperial	American
Small lamb chops	2	2	2
Oil	5 ml	1 tsp	1 tsp
Grated lemon rind	2.5 ml	½ tsp	½ tsp
Pinch of brown sugar			
Pinch of ground ginger			
Salt and freshly ground black pepper			

method

1. Place the chops in a dish. Mix the oil with the lemon rind, sugar, ginger, salt and pepper and pour over the chops. Cover and leave to stand for 2 hours, turning once or twice.

2. Preheat a browning dish according to the manufacturer's instructions. Add the chops and microwave on High for 3-4 minutes until cooked through, turning and basting with the marinade once or twice during cooking.

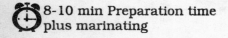 8-10 min Preparation time
plus marinating

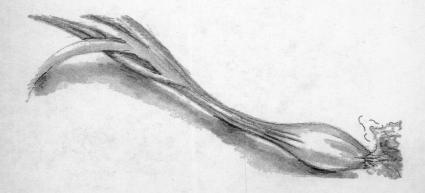

ORIENTAL LAMB

ingredients	Metric	Imperial	American
Oil	5 ml	1 tsp	1 tsp
Shallot, chopped	1	1	1
Celery stick, chopped	½	½	½
Carrot, chopped	½	½	½
Lean lamb, cubed	100 g	4 oz	¼ lb
Canned tomatoes	100 g	4 oz	¼ lb
Tomato purée (paste)	10 ml	2 tsp	2 tsp
Wine vinegar	10 ml	2 tsp	2 tsp
Pinch of sugar			
Chicken stock	75 ml	5 tbsp	5 tbsp
Salt and freshly ground black pepper			

method

1. Place the oil, onion, celery and carrot in a dish and microwave on High for 1 minute.

2. Add the meat, stir well, cover and microwave on High for 1 minute.

3. Add the remaining ingredients, cover and microwave on High for 8-9 minutes, stirring once or twice during cooking. Leave to stand for 4 minutes before serving.

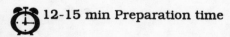 12-15 min Preparation time

LIVER AND ONIONS

ingredients	Metric	Imperial	American
Onions, sliced	75 g	3 oz	6 tbsp
Oil	15 ml	1 tbsp	1 tbsp
Lambs' liver, sliced	100 g	4 oz	¼ lb
Plain (all-purpose) flour	10 ml	2 tsp	2 tsp

method

1. Put the onions and half the oil in a dish and microwave on High for 2 minutes until softened.

2. Heat a browning dish according to the manufacturer's instructions. Add the remaining oil and heat for 30 seconds.

3. Dip the liver in flour, add to the hot oil and microwave on High for 1-2 minutes. Turn the liver over, add the onions, and microwave on High for a further 2-3 minutes until cooked through.

 8-10 min Preparation time

LAMB CURRY

ingredients	Metric	Imperial	American
Oil	5 ml	1 tsp	1 tsp
Shallot, chopped	1	1	1
Garlic clove, crushed	1	1	1
Ground coriander	2.5 ml	½ tsp	½ tsp
Pinch of chilli powder			
Pinch of ground cumin			
Pinch of ground cardamom			
Pinch of ground cloves			
Plain (all-purpose) flour	10 ml	2 tsp	2 tsp
Lamb, cubed	100 g	4 oz	¼ lb
Stock	150 ml	¼ pt	⅔ cup
Ground turmeric	2.5 ml	½ tsp	½ tsp
Salt and freshly ground black pepper			
Squeeze of lemon juice			

method

1. Put the oil, shallot and garlic in a casserole and microwave on High for 1 minute.

2. Blend in all the spices except the turmeric and microwave on High for 45 seconds.

3. Stir in the flour, meat and stock, cover and microwave on High for 3 minutes then on Low for 10-15 minutes until the meat is tender.

4. Stir in the turmeric, salt, pepper and lemon juice and serve with rice.

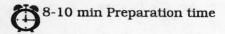 8-10 min Preparation time

LAMB AND AUBERGINE CASSEROLE

ingredients	Metric	Imperial	American
Small aubergine (eggplant)	1	1	1
Salt			
Olive oil	10 ml	2 tsp	2 tsp
Lean minced (ground) lamb	225 g	8 oz	½ lb
Shallot, finely chopped	1	1	1
Button mushrooms	50 g	2 oz	½ cup
Pinch of dried rosemary			
Pinch of dried thyme			
Garlic clove, crushed	½	½	½
Salt and freshly ground black pepper			
Beef stock	75 ml	5 tbsp	5 tbsp
Pinch of cornflour (cornstarch)			
Tomato purée (paste)	15 ml	1 tbsp	1 tbsp
Egg	1	1	1

method

1. Slice the aubergine in half lengthways and slash the pulp deeply. Sprinkle with salt and leave to stand for 30 minutes.

2. Squeeze the moisture from the aubergines and brush the cut surfaces with oil. Microwave on High for 2-3 minutes.

3. Scoop the pulp into a bowl and reserve the skins. Chop the pulp coarsely then microwave on High for 1 minute. Line an oiled casserole with the aubergine skins.

4. Place the lamb in a separate bowl and microwave on High for 2 minutes. Drain and discard the juices.

5. Place the shallot, mushrooms, herbs, garlic, salt and pepper in a bowl and microwave on High for 2 minutes.

6. Blend the stock and cornflour and microwave on High for 30 seconds.

7. Mix together all the prepared and remaining ingredients and spoon into the aubergine shells. Cover and microwave on High for 4-5 minutes until cooked through. Serve with tomato sauce.

16-20 min Preparation time
plus resting

LAMB AND COURGETTE BAKE

ingredients	Metric	Imperial	American
Minced (ground) lamb	50 g	2 oz	⅛ lb
Shallot, chopped	1	1	1
Garlic clove, crushed	½	½	½
Small courgette (zucchini), thinly sliced	1	1	1
Passata (sieved tomatoes)	175 g	6 oz	¾ cup
Pinch of dried marjoram			
Pinch of dried oregano			
Pinch of sugar			
Salt and freshly ground black pepper			

method

1. Mix together the lamb, shallot and garlic and microwave on High for 1-3 minutes until the meat is no longer pink. Drain.

2. Stir in the remaining ingredients, cover with greaseproof (waxed) paper and microwave on High for 4-7 minutes until the sauce is hot and bubbly and the courgette is tender, stirring several times during cooking.

3. Cover and leave to stand for 2 minutes. Serve with rice.

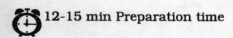 12-15 min Preparation time

PORK MEATBALLS

ingredients	Metric	Imperial	American
Minced (ground) pork	100 g	4 oz	¼ lb
Minced (ground) ham	100 g	4 oz	¼ lb
Dry breadcrumbs	30 ml	2 tbsp	2 tbsp
Shallot, chopped	1	1	1
French mustard	1.5 ml	¼ tsp	¼ tsp
Salt and freshly ground black pepper			
Small egg, beaten	1	1	1

method

1. Mix all the ingredients together in a bowl, adding enough egg to bind the mixture together. Shape into 5 cm/2 in balls and place on a plate lined with greaseproof (waxed) paper.

2. Cover with greaseproof (waxed) paper and microwave on High for 5-6 minutes until cooked through, rearranging at least once during cooking.

 8-10 min Preparation time

PORK STIR-FRY

ingredients	Metric	Imperial	American
Oil	5 ml	1 tsp	1 tsp
Pork fillet, cubed	100 g	4 oz	¼ lb
Garlic clove, crushed	½	½	½
Spring onion (scallion), chopped	1	1	1
Celery stick, chopped	½	½	½
Cornflour (cornstarch)	5 ml	1 tsp	1 tsp
Soy sauce	15 ml	1 tbsp	1 tbsp
Sweet sherry	5 ml	1 tsp	1 tsp
Water	15 ml	1 tbsp	1 tbsp
Pinch of ground ginger			
Salt and freshly ground black pepper			
Beansprouts	50 g	2 oz	⅛ lb

method

1. Mix the oil, pork, garlic, spring onion and celery and microwave on High for 2-3 minutes, stirring once during cooking.

2. Blend the cornflour with the soy sauce, sherry and water and add to the pan with the ginger, salt and pepper. Microwave on High for 1-2 minutes.

3. Stir in the beansprouts and microwave on High for 45-60 seconds until all the ingredients are well blended and heated through. Serve with rice.

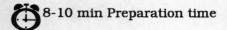 8-10 min Preparation time

PORK AND PEPPER HOT POT

ingredients	Metric	Imperial	American
Belly pork, cubed	25 g	1 oz	2 tbsp
Onion, chopped	1/2	1/2	1/2
Red (bell) pepper, chopped	1/4	1/4	1/4
Garlic clove, crushed	1/2	1/2	1/2
Potato, peeled and cubed	1	1	1
Chicken stock	150 ml	1/4 pt	2/3 cup
Canned borlotti beans, drained and rinsed	100 g	4 oz	1/4 lb
Pinch of sugar			
Pinch of grated nutmeg			
Freshly ground black pepper			

method

1. Put the pork, onion, pepper and garlic into a casserole dish, cover and microwave on High for 3-5 minutes until the vegetables are tender, stirring occasionally during cooking.

2. Add the remaining ingredients, cover and microwave on High for 4 minutes, stirring occasionally.

3. Reduce the power to Medium and microwave for 8-10 minutes until the vegetables and meat are tender, stirring several times during cooking.

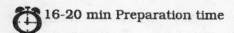 16-20 min Preparation time

SAUSAGE AND APPLE BAKE

ingredients	Metric	Imperial	American
Pork sausages	100 g	4 oz	1/4 lb
Small onion, thinly sliced	1	1	1
Eating apple, peeled and thinly sliced	1	1	1
Sauce:			
Shallot, chopped	1	1	1
Butter or margarine	10 ml	2 tsp	2 tsp
Plain (all-purpose) flour	5 ml	1 tsp	1 tsp
French mustard	2.5 ml	1/2 tsp	1/2 tsp
Few drops of Worcestershire sauce			
Few drops of tabasco sauce			
Dark soft brown sugar	5 ml	1 tsp	1 tsp
Pinch of salt			
Malt vinegar	10 ml	2 tsp	2 tsp
Tomato juice	75 ml	5 tbsp	5 tbsp

method

1. Prick the sausages with a fork and arrange in a shallow dish. Cover and microwave on High for 1½-2 minutes. Remove from the dish.

2. Add the onions, cover and microwave on High for 2 minutes. Add the apples and toss together gently. Microwave on High for about 1 minute.

3. To make the sauce, place the shallot and butter or margarine in a small bowl and microwave on High for 1-2 minutes. Stir in the flour then blend in all the remaining ingredients.

4. Microwave on High for 3-4 minutes, stirring twice during cooking.

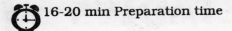

5. Pour the sauce over the sausages and microwave on High for 1-2 minutes until hot. Serve with crusty bread and a green salad.

16-20 min Preparation time

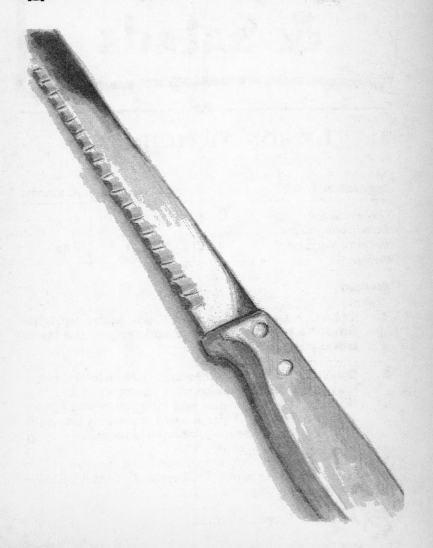

VEGETABLES & SALADS

LEMON ARTICHOKES

ingredients	Metric	Imperial	American
Globe artichoke	1	1	1
Lemon, thinly sliced	½	½	½
Butter or margarine	25 g	1 oz	2 tbsp

method

1. Trim the artichoke so that it will stand upright. Snip the tips of the leaves and remove the lower leaves. Rinse well.

2. Quarter the lemon slices and tuck into the outer leaves of the artichoke with the rind at the top. Wrap in microwave film and microwave on High for 3-4 minutes until the lower leaves can be easily pulled off the base and the base is tender.

3. Put the butter in a small bowl and microwave on High for 20 seconds until melted. Serve with the artichoke for dipping.

 8-10 min Preparation time

AUBERGINE BAKE

ingredients	Metric	Imperial	American
Aubergines (eggplants), peeled and sliced	100 g	4 oz	¼ lb
Shallot, chopped	1	1	1
Butter or margarine	10 ml	2 tsp	2 tsp
Canned chopped tomatoes, drained	100 g	4 oz	¼ lb
Garlic clove, crushed	½	½	½
Salt and freshly ground black pepper			
Canned sweetcorn, drained	50 g	2 oz	½ cup

method

1. Place the aubergines, shallot and butter or margarine in a casserole, cover and microwave on High for 2 minutes until soft.

2. Stir in the remaining ingredients, cover and microwave on High for 3-5 minutes until well blended and tender. Leave to stand for 1 minute before serving.

 8-10 min Preparation time

SPICED BEANS WITH CORIANDER

ingredients	Metric	Imperial	American
Green beans	100 g	4 oz	¼ lb
Red chilli, chopped	½	½	½
Butter or margarine	15 ml	1 tbsp	1 tbsp
Chopped fresh coriander	5 ml	1 tsp	1 tsp
Lime or lemon juice	5 ml	1 tsp	1 tsp
Pinch of sugar			
Pinch of salt			

method

1. Top and tail the beans and mix with the remaining ingredients. Cover and microwave on High for 4-6 minutes until the beans are just tender but still crisp, stirring once during cooking.

2. Leave to stand for 1 minute and toss well before serving.

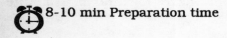 8-10 min Preparation time

BROCCOLI WITH PIQUANT CHEESE SAUCE

ingredients	Metric	Imperial	American
Broccoli florets	100 g	4 oz	¼ lb
Water	30 ml	2 tbsp	2 tbsp
Butter or margarine	10 ml	2 tsp	2 tsp
Plain (all-purpose) flour	10 ml	2 tsp	2 tsp
Milk	150 ml	¼ pt	⅔ cup
French mustard	5 ml	1 tsp	1 tsp
Salt and freshly ground black pepper			
Strong Cheddar cheese, grated	50 g	2 oz	½ cup

method

1. Arrange the broccoli in a dish and spoon over the water. Cover and microwave on High for 4-5 minutes until just tender, rearranging once during cooking. Drain.

2. Place the butter or margarine in a jug and microwave on High for 10 seconds until melted. Stir in the flour then blend in the milk and mustard.

3. Microwave on High for 45 seconds then stir well. Microwave on High for 45 seconds until the sauce is smooth and coats the back of a spoon. Season with salt and pepper and stir in most of the cheese.

4. Pour the sauce over the broccoli and sprinkle with the remaining cheese. Microwave on High for about 1 minute until the cheese melts.

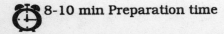 8-10 min Preparation time

BROCCOLI AND MUSHROOMS

ingredients	Metric	Imperial	American
Broccoli florets	100 g	4 oz	¼ lb
Button mushrooms	100 g	4 oz	¼ lb
Water	45 ml	3 tbsp	3 tbsp
Olive oil	30 ml	2 tbsp	2 tbsp
Red wine vinegar	15 ml	1 tbsp	1 tbsp
Dried oregano	2.5 ml	½ tsp	½ tsp
Salt and freshly ground black pepper			

method

1. Place the broccoli, mushrooms and water in a bowl, cover and microwave on High for about 1 minute until just beginning to soften but still crisp. Drain and rinse in cold water.

2. Whisk together the oil, wine vinegar and oregano and season with salt and pepper. Pour over the vegetables and toss together well. Cover and chill before serving.

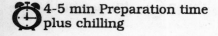
4-5 min Preparation time
plus chilling

ORIENTAL SPICED CARROTS

ingredients	Metric	Imperial	American
Carrots, sliced	2	2	2
Green (bell) pepper, chopped	½	½	½
Shallot, chopped	1	1	1
Water	15 ml	1 tbsp	1 tbsp
Canned water chestnuts, drained	50 g	2 oz	4 tbsp
Tomato soup	60 ml	4 tbsp	4 tbsp
Pinch of sugar			
Few drops of wine vinegar			
Few drops of soy sauce			
Salt and freshly ground black pepper			

method

1. Put the carrots, pepper, shallot and water into a casserole, cover and microwave on High for 3-4 minutes until the carrots are just tender, stirring once during cooking.

2. Stir in the remaining ingredients, cover and microwave on High for 1-2 minutes until heated through. Serve hot or cold.

 8-10 min Preparation time

CARROTS WITH MINT

ingredients	Metric	Imperial	American
Carrots, cut into strips	2	2	2
Dry white wine	15 ml	1 tbsp	1 tbsp
Butter or margarine	25 g	1 oz	2 tbsp
Chopped fresh mint	5 ml	1 tsp	1 tsp
Salt and freshly ground black pepper			

method

1. Place the carrots and wine in a bowl, cover and microwave on High for 2-3 minutes until just tender. Drain.

2. Place the butter or margarine in a bowl and microwave on High for 20 seconds until softened. Mix in the mint and season with salt and pepper.

3. Spoon the butter over the carrots and toss together before serving.

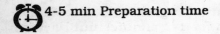 4-5 min Preparation time

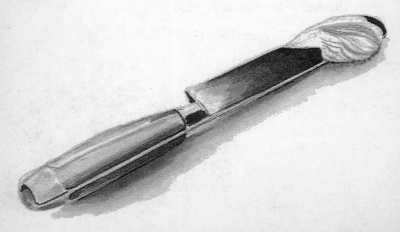

MUSHROOM WITH SALAMI

ingredients	Metric	Imperial	American
Butter or margarine	15 ml	1 tbsp	1 tbsp
Shallot, finely chopped	1	1	1
Garlic clove, crushed	½	½	½
Mushrooms, sliced	50 g	2 oz	½ cup
Salami, diced	25 g	1 oz	2 tbsp
Pinch of dried basil			
Pinch of chopped fresh parsley			
Dry white wine	5 ml	1 tsp	1 tsp
Single (light) cream	45 ml	3 tbsp	3 tbsp
Salt and freshly ground black pepper			

method

1. Place the butter or margarine, shallot and garlic in a bowl and microwave on High for 1 minute.

2. Add the mushrooms and salami and microwave on High for 45 seconds.

3. Stir in the remaining ingredients, cover and microwave on High for 1-2 minutes until the sauce has thickened.

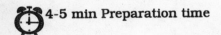 4-5 min Preparation time

POTATO LYONNAISE

ingredients	Metric	Imperial	American
Potatoes, thinly sliced	100 g	4 oz	¼ lb
Butter or margarine, melted	15 ml	1 tbsp	1 tbsp
Plain (all-purpose) flour	10 ml	2 tsp	2 tsp
Milk or single (light) cream	90 ml	6 tbsp	6 tbsp
Salt and freshly ground black pepper			
Chopped fresh chives	5 ml	1 tsp	1 tsp

method

1. Arrange the potatoes in a casserole. Mix together the butter or margarine, flour, milk or cream and salt and pepper. Pour over the potatoes and sprinkle with chives.

2. Cover and microwave on Medium for about 8 minutes until the potatoes are just soft. Leave to stand for 2 minutes before serving.

 12-15 min Preparation time

JACKET POTATOES

ingredients	Metric	Imperial	American
Baking potato, 175 g/6 oz	1	1	1

method

1. Prick the potato skin all over with a fork and wrap the potato in kitchen paper.

2. Microwave on High for 5-6 minutes.

3. Wrap the potato in kitchen foil, shiny side in, and leave to stand for 5 minutes.

4. Cut a cross in the top of the potato and arrange on a warm serving plate. Top with the filling of your choice (see following recipes) and microwave on High for about 1 minute to heat through.

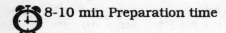 8-10 min Preparation time

VEGETABLE-FILLED POTATO

ingredients	Metric	Imperial	American
Large baked potato	1	1	1
Milk	30 ml	2 tbsp	2 tbsp
Butter or margarine	15 ml	1 tbsp	1 tbsp
Frozen peas, thawed	30 ml	2 tbsp	2 tbsp
Small carrot, grated	½	½	½
Spring onion (scallion), finely chopped	1	1	1
Water	15 ml	1 tbsp	1 tbsp
Salt and freshly ground black pepper			

method

1. Cut the baked potato in half lengthways and scoop out the centre. Mash the potato with the milk and butter or margarine.

2. Place the peas, carrot, spring onion and water in a bowl and microwave on High for 1 minute until soft. Drain.

3. Stir the vegetables into the mashed potato and season with salt and pepper. Spoon the mixture into the potato skins. Microwave on High for 3-4 minutes until hot.

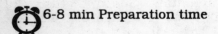 6-8 min Preparation time

TUNA POTATO

ingredients	Metric	Imperial	American
Butter or margarine	15 ml	1 tbsp	1 tbsp
Spring onion (scallion), sliced	1	1	1
Celery stick, chopped	½	½	½
Chopped fresh parsley	5 ml	1 tsp	1 tsp
Large baked potato	1	1	1
Soured (dairy sour) cream	15 ml	2 tbsp	2 tbsp
Milk	10 ml	2 tsp	2 tsp
Chopped fresh chives	2.5 ml	½ tsp	½ tsp
Salt and freshly ground black pepper			
Canned tuna, drained	50 g	2 oz	scant ¼ cup
Cheddar cheese, grated	30 ml	2 tbsp	2 tbsp

method

1. Put the butter or margarine, spring onion, celery and parsley in a bowl and microwave on High for 1-2 minutes until tender, stirring once.

2. Slice the potato in half lengthways and scoop out the flesh. Stir the potato into the vegetables.

3. Mix in the cream, milk, chives, salt and pepper and beat until smooth and fluffy. Stir in the tuna and half the cheese. Pile the mixture back into the potato shells and sprinkle with the remaining cheese.

4. Microwave on High for 1-2 minutes until heated through and the cheese has melted.

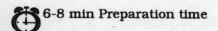 6-8 min Preparation time

SOUFFLÉ POTATOES

ingredients	Metric	Imperial	American
Large baked potato	1	1	1
Egg, beaten	1	1	1
Milk (optional)	5 ml	1 tsp	1 tsp
Pinch of cayenne pepper			
Salt and freshly ground black pepper			
Grated Cheddar cheese	30 ml	2 tbsp	2 tbsp

method

1. Cut a horizontal slice off the top of the potato and scoop out the inside flesh, leaving a hollow shell.

2. Mix the potato flesh with the egg and beat until smooth and soft, adding the milk if necessary. Season with cayenne, salt and pepper.

3. Pile the mixture back into the potato shell and top with the cheese. Microwave on High for about 1 minute until the potato is hot and the cheese has melted.

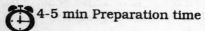 4-5 min Preparation time

CHILLI-SPICED POTATO

ingredients	Metric	Imperial	American
Butter or margarine	15 ml	1 tbsp	1 tbsp
Medium potato, quartered	1	1	1
Chilli powder	1.5 ml	¼ tsp	¼ tsp
Pinch of dried oregano			
Pinch of ground cumin			

method

1. Put the butter or margarine into a casserole and microwave on High for 40 seconds until the butter melts.

2. Add the potato and turn to coat in the butter. Mix together the remaining ingredients and sprinkle over the potato. Cover and microwave on High for 3-4 minutes until the potato is tender, rearranging once or twice during cooking.

3. Cover and leave to stand for 2 minutes before serving.

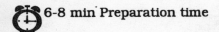 6-8 min Preparation time

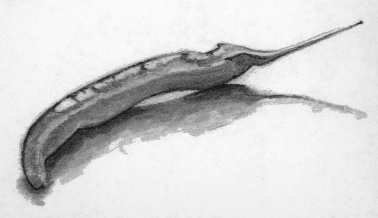

ITALIAN-STYLE RED PEPPER

ingredients	Metric	Imperial	American
Red (bell) pepper, cut into strips	1	1	1
Small onion, sliced	1	1	1
Garlic clove, crushed	½	½	½
Pinch of dried oregano			
Olive oil	10 ml	2 tsp	2 tsp
White wine vinegar	5 ml	1 tsp	1 tsp

method

1. Place all the ingredients in a casserole dish, cover and microwave on High for 3-4 minutes until the peppers are just tender, stirring once or twice during cooking.

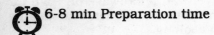 6-8 min Preparation time

TOMATO PLATTER

ingredients	Metric	Imperial	American
Tomato, sliced	1	1	1
Cherry tomatoes	4	4	4
Spring onion (scallion), sliced	1	1	1
Butter or margarine	10 ml	2 tsp	2 tsp
Chopped fresh basil	5 ml	1 tsp	1 tsp
Pinch of soft brown sugar			
Pinch of salt			

method

1. Arrange the tomatoes on a plate and sprinkle with the spring onion. Cover with microwave film and microwave on High for 1-2 minutes until the tomatoes are just warm.

2. Place the butter or margarine in a bowl and microwave on High for 10 seconds until melted. Stir in the basil, sugar and salt. Drizzle over the tomatoes and serve at once.

 4-5 min Preparation time

VEGETABLE DELIGHT

ingredients	Metric	Imperial	American
Butter or margarine	10 ml	2 tsp	2 tsp
Courgette (zucchini), thinly sliced	1	1	1
Shallot, chopped	1	1	1
Green (bell) pepper, chopped	½	½	½
Small carrot, sliced	1	1	1
Canned chopped tomatoes, drained	175 g	6 oz	6 oz
Mushrooms, sliced	25 g	1 oz	¼ cup
Pinch of dried oregano			
Pinch of dried basil			
Pinch of dried thyme			
Salt and freshly ground black pepper			

method

1. Put the butter or margarine, courgette, shallot, pepper and carrot into a casserole, cover and microwave on High for 3-5 minutes until tender, stirring once during cooking.

2. Stir in the remaining ingredients, cover and microwave on Medium for 2-4 minutes until the flavours are blended, stirring once during cooking.

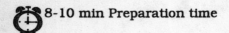 8-10 min Preparation time

SPINACH AND FRUIT SALAD

ingredients	Metric	Imperial	American
Bacon (rashers) slices, rinded and chopped	2	2	2
White wine vinegar	30 ml	2 tbsp	2 tbsp
Soft brown sugar	5 ml	1 tsp	1 tsp
Pinch of salt			
Spinach leaves, torn into pieces	50 g	2 oz	$\frac{1}{8}$ lb
Nectarine, cut into wedges	1	1	1
Plum, cut into wedges	1	1	1

method

1. Place the bacon in a casserole and cover with kitchen paper. Microwave on High for 2-3 minutes until crisp.

2. Drain off all but 10 ml/2 tsp of the fat. Stir in the wine vinegar, sugar and salt and mix thoroughly. Add the remaining ingredients and toss well to coat.

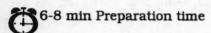 6-8 min Preparation time

CURRIED TURKEY SALAD

ingredients	Metric	Imperial	American
Turkey breast portion, about 225 g/8 oz/½ lb	1	1	1
Carrot, cut into strips	1	1	1
Water	15 ml	1 tbsp	1 tbsp
Honey	5 ml	1 tsp	1 tsp
Pinch of curry powder			
Freshly ground black pepper			
Long-grain rice	75 g	3 oz	scant ⅓ cup
A few lettuce leaves			
A few raisins			
Dressing:			
Mayonnaise	45 ml	3 tbsp	3 tbsp
Few drops of lemon juice			
Honey	2.5 ml	½ tsp	½ tsp
Curry powder	2.5 ml	½ tsp	½ tsp
Salt			

method

1. Cut the turkey into 2.5 cm/1 in slices across the grain.

2. Place the carrot in a bowl with the water, honey, curry powder and pepper and toss until coated. Cover and microwave on Medium for 1-3 minutes until the carrots are tender. Remove them from the liquid with a slotted spoon.

3. Add the turkey to the liquid, cover and microwave on Medium for 3-5 minutes until no longer pink. Drain.

4. Meanwhile, cook the rice in boiling salted water on a conventional oven. Drain well.

5. Mix together all the dressing ingredients.

6. Arrange the lettuce on a plate and top with the rice. Arrange the turkey on top and sprinkle with the carrots and raisins. Spoon over the dressing and serve.

 12-15 min Preparation time

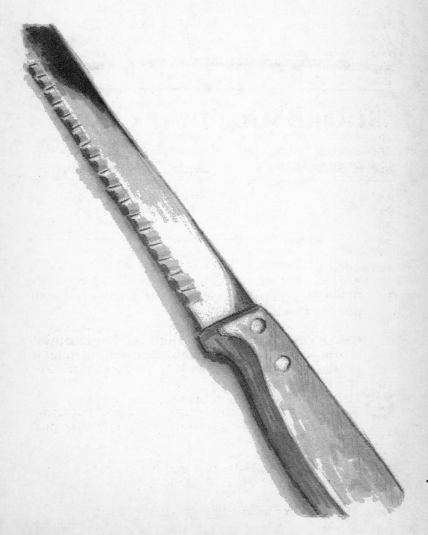

PASTA & RICE

SIMPLE MICROWAVE PASTA

ingredients	Metric	Imperial	American
Pasta Boiling water Salt	*100 g*	*4 oz*	*¼ lb*

method

1. Place the pasta in a casserole and cover with plenty of boiling salted water.

2. Cover and microwave on High for 3-4 minutes, stirring once during cooking. Stir well, then leave to stand for 3-4 minutes.

 12-15 min Preparation time

TOMATO AND BACON MACARONI

ingredients

ingredients	Metric	Imperial	American
Macaroni	50 g	2 oz	1/2 cup
Bacon (rashers) slices, rinded and chopped	2	2	2
Tomato purée (paste)	30 ml	2 tbsp	2 tbsp
Passata (sieved tomatoes)	120 ml	4 fl oz	1/2 cup
Chopped fresh parsley	10 ml	2 tsp	2 tsp
Pinch of sugar			
Salt and freshly ground black pepper			
Grated Parmesan cheese	15 ml	1 tbsp	1 tbsp

method

1. Cook the macaroni as directed on the packet. Rinse and drain.

2. Place the bacon in a casserole and microwave on High for 2-3 minutes until crisp. Drain and reserve 10 ml/2 tsp of the fat.

3. Stir the tomato purée, passata, parsley, sugar, salt and pepper into the casserole, cover and microwave on High for 2-3 minutes until the flavours are blended.

4. Stir in the cooked macaroni and sprinkle with the cheese. Cover and microwave on High for 1-2 minutes until hot.

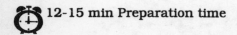 12-15 min Preparation time

SIMPLE MICROWAVE RICE

ingredients	Metric	Imperial	American
Long-grain rice	100 g	4 oz	¼ lb
Hot water	250 ml	8 fl oz	1 cup
Oil	5 ml	1 tsp	1 tsp
Salt			

method

1. Measure the rice in a cup and pour it into a large casserole. Measure twice the volume of hot water and stir into the rice with the oil and salt. The dish should only be half full.

2. Cover and microwave on Medium for 3-5 minutes until the rice is just tender. Stir well then leave to stand for 5 minutes.

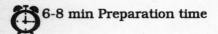 6-8 min Preparation time

OREGANO RICE

ingredients	Metric	Imperial	American
Chicken stock	120 ml	4 fl oz	½ cup
Long-grain rice	25 g	1 oz	⅛ cup
Small shallot, chopped	1	1	1
Butter or margarine	10 ml	2 tsp	2 tsp
Dried oregano	1.5 ml	¼ tsp	¼ tsp
Salt and freshly ground black pepper			

method

1. Put all the ingredients into a casserole and mix well. Cover and microwave on High for 2 minutes.

2. Microwave on Medium for 3-5 minutes until the liquid has been absorbed and the rice is tender.

3. Leave to stand, covered, for 2 minutes then stir with a fork before serving.

 8-10 min Preparation time

SAUCES

CIDER AND RAISIN SAUCE

ingredients	Metric	Imperial	American
Brown sugar	25 g	1 oz	2 tbsp
Cornflour (cornstarch)	5 ml	1 tsp	1 tsp
Dry cider	75 ml	5 tbsp	5 tbsp
Squeeze of lemon juice			
Raisins	25 g	1 oz	3 tbsp
Pinch of ground cinnamon			

method

1. Mix all the ingredients together until well blended. Microwave on High for 1-2 minutes until thickened, stirring occasionally.

2. Serve with ham or pork dishes.

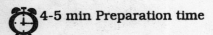 4-5 min Preparation time

CHEESE SAUCE

ingredients	Metric	Imperial	American
Butter or margarine	15 ml	1 tbsp	1 tbsp
Plain (all-purpose) flour	15 ml	1 tbsp	1 tbsp
Pinch of cayenne pepper			
Pinch of mustard			
Salt and freshly ground black pepper			
Milk	150 ml	¼ pt	⅔ cup
Cheddar cheese, grated	25 g	1 oz	¼ cup

method

1. Put the butter or margarine in a bowl and microwave on High for 30 seconds until melted.

2. Stir in the flour, cayenne, mustard, salt and pepper then blend in the milk. Microwave on High for 2-3 minutes until the mixture thickens and bubbles, stirring once or twice during cooking.

3. Stir in the cheese until melted.

4. Serve with fish, pasta or vegetables.

4-5 min Preparation time

CREAM SAUCE

ingredients	Metric	Imperial	American
Milk	150 ml	¼ pt	⅔ cup
Pinch of grated nutmeg			
Bay leaf	½	½	½
Butter or margarine	10 ml	2 tsp	2 tsp
Plain (all-purpose) flour	10 ml	2 tsp	2 tsp
Salt and freshly ground black pepper			
Double (heavy) cream	15 ml	1 tbsp	1 tbsp

method

1. Put the milk, nutmeg and bay leaf in a bowl and microwave on High for 1-2 minutes until hot but not boiling. Discard the bay leaf.

2. Put the butter or margarine in a bowl and microwave on High for 30 seconds until melted.

3. Stir the flour into the butter and season with salt and pepper. Blend in the hot milk. Microwave on Medium for 1-2 minutes until the mixture thickens and bubbles, stirring occasionally during cooking. Stir in the cream.

4. Serve with seafood, vegetables or chicken.

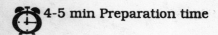 4-5 min Preparation time

CREAMY ORANGE SAUCE

ingredients	Metric	Imperial	American
Butter or margarine	15 ml	1 tbsp	1 tbsp
Spring onion (scallion), sliced	1	1	1
Chopped fresh parsley	5 ml	1 tsp	1 tsp
Grated orange rind	2.5 ml	½ tsp	½ tsp
Plain (all-purpose) flour	5 ml	1 tsp	1 tsp
Pinch of mustard powder			
Milk	75 ml	5 tbsp	5 tbsp
Orange juice	15 ml	1 tbsp	1 tbsp
Salt and freshly ground black pepper			

method

1. Put the butter or margarine, spring onion, parsley and orange rind into a bowl and microwave on High for 1 minute until the butter melts.

2. Stir in the flour and mustard then blend in the milk. Microwave on High for 1-2 minutes until the mixture thickens and bubbles, stirring occasionally during cooking.

3. Stir in the orange juice and season with salt and pepper.

4. Serve with fish or chicken.

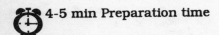 4-5 min Preparation time

VEGETABLE SAUCE

ingredients	Metric	Imperial	American
Tomato, cut into wedges	1	1	1
Carrot, grated	½	½	½
Small shallot, chopped	1	1	1
Chopped fresh parsley	15 ml	1 tbsp	1 tbsp
Garlic clove, crushed	½	½	½
Tomato purée (paste)	10 ml	2 tsp	2 tsp
Pinch of sugar			
Pinch of dried sage			
Pinch of grated nutmeg			
Salt and freshly ground black pepper			

method

1. Purée the tomato, carrot, shallot, parsley and garlic in a food processor until smooth.

2. Pour into a casserole and stir in the remaining ingredients. Microwave on High for 3-5 minutes until slightly thickened, stirring once or twice during cooking.

3. Serve with fish, chicken or turkey.

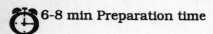 6-8 min Preparation time

138

CARAMEL SAUCE

ingredients	Metric	Imperial	American
Mars bar	1	1	1
Milk	30 ml	2 tbsp	2 tbsp

method

1. Chop the Mars bar and place in a jug with the milk. Microwave on High for 1-2 minutes, stirring once or twice until melted.

2. Serve hot with ice cream or plain sponges.

 4-5 min Preparation time

LEMON SAUCE

ingredients	Metric	Imperial	American
Grated rind and juice of lemon	½	½	½
Caster (superfine) sugar	5 ml	1 tsp	1 tsp
Cornflour (cornstarch)	5 ml	1 tsp	1 tsp
Water	150 ml	¼ pt	⅔ cup

method

1. Mix together all the ingredients until smooth. Microwave on High for 1-2 minutes until hot, stirring once during cooking.

2. Serve hot with sponge puddings or ice cream.

4-5 min Preparation time

DESSERTS

CHOCOLATE BANANA

ingredients	Metric	Imperial	American
Banana	1	1	1
Milk or plain (semi-sweet) chocolate	100 g	4 oz	¼ lb
Golden (light corn) syrup	15 ml	1 tbsp	1 tbsp
Chopped mixed nuts	30 ml	2 tbsp	2 tbsp

method

1. Slice the banana in half lengthways and place in a bowl.

2. Break the chocolate into pieces and place in a bowl with the syrup. Microwave on Medium for 1-3 minutes until melted, stirring occasionally until smooth.

3. Spoon the chocolate over the banana and sprinkle with the nuts. Leave to cool then chill until the chocolate is firm. Serve with ice cream.

6-8 min Preparation time
plus chilling

SPICED PEARS

ingredients	Metric	Imperial	American
Pear	1	1	1
Red wine	75 ml	5 tbsp	5 tbsp
Water	75 ml	5 tbsp	5 tbsp
Sugar	15 ml	1 tbsp	1 tbsp
Small piece of cinnamon stick			
Clove	1	1	1
Pinch of grated nutmeg			
Piece of lemon rind			
Few drops of lemon juice			
Flaked almonds	15 ml	1 tbsp	1 tbsp

method

1. Peel the pear carefully, leaving the fruit whole with the stalk.

2. Put the wine, water, sugar, spices, lemon rind and juice in a bowl and microwave on High for 2 minutes.

3. Stand the pear in the liquid and microwave on High for 1-2 minutes until softened. Leave to stand for 2 minutes, spooning the syrup over the pear a few times.

4. Remove the spices and lemon rind. Sprinkle with almonds and serve with cream.

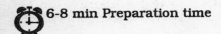 6-8 min Preparation time

PEACH MOUSSE

ingredients	Metric	Imperial	American
Canned peaches	100 g	4 oz	¼ lb
Egg, separated	1	1	1
Sugar	25 g	1 oz	2 tbsp
Pinch of salt			
Apricot jam	10 ml	2 tsp	2 tsp
Lemon juice	10 ml	2 tsp	2 tsp
Whipping (heavy) cream	100 ml	3½ fl oz	6½ tbsp

method

1. Purée the peaches with a little of their juice in a food processor. Set aside.

2. Beat the egg yolk, sugar and salt until thick and pale yellow. Blend in the jam, lemon juice and remaining peach juice. Microwave on Medium for 5-7 minutes until thick, stirring twice. Mix in the puréed peaches. Leave to cool.

3. Beat the egg whites until stiff then fold into the fruit mixture. Whisk the cream until stiff and then fold into the mixture. Pour into a mould and chill before serving.

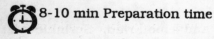 8-10 min Preparation time

STRAWBERRY AND RHUBARB CRUMBLE

ingredients	Metric	Imperial	American
Rhubarb, cut into chunks	100 g	4 oz	¼ lb
Plain (all-purpose) flour	10 ml	2 tsp	2 tsp
Strawberries, sliced	100 g	4 oz	¼ lb
Topping:			
Rolled oats	15 ml	1 tbsp	1 tbsp
Plain (all-purpose) flour	15 ml	1 tbsp	1 tbsp
Brown sugar	30 ml	2 tbsp	2 tbsp
Granulated sugar	15 ml	1 tbsp	1 tbsp
Pinch of ground cinnamon			
Pinch of grated nutmeg			
Butter or margarine, cubed	30 ml	2 tbsp	2 tbsp

method

1. Put the rhubarb into a casserole and sprinkle with the flour. Stir to coat. Cover and microwave on High for 3-4 minutes until tender, stirring once. Stir in the strawberries.

2. Mix together the topping ingredients and rub in the butter until the mixture resembles breadcrumbs.

3. Sprinkle the topping over the fruit and microwave on Medium for 4-5 minutes until bubbly in the centre. Serve with cream or ice cream.

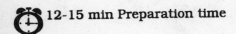 12-15 min Preparation time

ORANGE-GLAZED PINEAPPLE

ingredients	Metric	Imperial	American
Pineapple slices	3-4	3-4	3-4
Orange marmalade	30 ml	2 tbsp	2 tbsp
Pineapple or orange juice	15 ml	1 tbsp	1 tbsp

method

1. Mix together the marmalade and pineapple or orange juice. Microwave on High for 30 seconds until melted. Stir until smooth.

2. Brush the pineapple slices with the marmalade mixture and microwave on High for about 1 minute until hot, basting with the marmalade.

 4-5 min Preparation time

CHOCOLATE SPONGE PUDDING

Serves 1-2

ingredients	Metric	Imperial	American
Soft margarine	50 g	2 oz	¼ cup
Caster (superfine) sugar	50 g	2 oz	¼ cup
Egg	1	1	1
Self-raising flour	50 g	2 oz	½ cup
Cocoa powder	25 g	1 oz	¼ cup
Baking powder	2.5 ml	½ tsp	½ tsp

method

1. Beat all the ingredients together until smooth and creamy.

2. Line a bowl with cling film, spoon in the mixture and smooth the top. Microwave on Medium for about 3 minutes until just cooked.

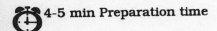 4-5 min Preparation time

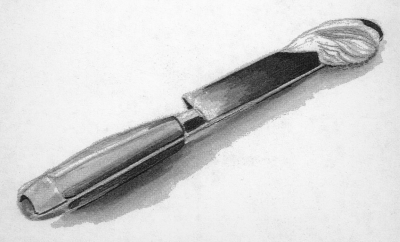

CHOCOLATE MOUSSE

ingredients

ingredients	Metric	Imperial	American
Plain chocolate	50 g	2 oz	⅛ lb
Strong black coffee	15 ml	1 tbsp	1 tbsp
Few drops of brandy			
Egg, separated	1	1	1

method

1. Mix the chocolate, coffee and brandy in a bowl and microwave on High for 45-60 seconds until melted. Stir well.

2. Blend in the egg yolks and leave to cool slightly.

3. Whisk the egg whites until stiff then fold into the mixture. Pour into a dish and leave to set in the refrigerator.

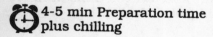 4-5 min Preparation time
plus chilling

SULTANA RICE PUDDING

ingredients	Metric	Imperial	American
Shortgrain rice	25 g	1 oz	2 tbsp
Milk	300 ml	½ pt	1¼ cups
Sugar	15 ml	1 tbsp	1 tbsp
Butter or margarine	15 ml	1 tbsp	1 tbsp
Single (light) cream	15 ml	1 tbsp	1 tbsp
Sultanas (golden raisins)	15 ml	1 tbsp	1 tbsp
Grated nutmeg			

method

1. Mix the rice, milk and sugar and dot with the butter. Cover and microwave on High for 1½ minutes then stir well.

2. Microwave on Medium for 8-10 minutes, stirring once during cooking. Leave to stand for 2 minutes then stir in the cream and sultanas and sprinkle with nutmeg.

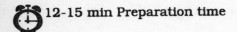 12-15 min Preparation time

BREAD AND BUTTER PUDDING

ingredients	Metric	Imperial	American
Slices bread and butter, cut into strips	2	2	2
Sultanas (golden raisins)	15 ml	1 tbsp	1 tbsp
Sugar	15 ml	1 tbsp	1 tbsp
Milk	120 ml	4 fl oz	½ cup
Small egg, beaten	1	1	1
Pinch of grated nutmeg			

method

1. Arrange the bread and butter strips in a dish, sprinkling the layers with sultanas and sugar.

2. Beat the milk and egg and pour over the bread. Sprinkle with nutmeg and leave to stand for 5 minutes.

3. Microwave on High for 2-4 minutes.

 12-15 min Preparation time

HONEY CRUNCH

ingredients	Metric	Imperial	American
Crisp eating (dessert) apples, peeled, cored and sliced	100 g	4 oz	¼ lb
Honey	30 ml	2 tbsp	2 tbsp
Butter or margarine	15 ml	1 tbsp	1 tbsp
Muesli	25 g	1 oz	2 tbsp

method

1. Arrange the apples in a dish and drizzle over half the honey.

2. Place the butter in a bowl and microwave on High for 20 seconds until melted. Stir in the remaining honey and the muesli and spoon over the apples. Cover and microwave on High for 4-5 minutes.

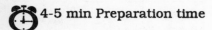 4-5 min Preparation time

Biscuits & Cakes

PEANUT BUTTER BISCUITS

Makes 18 biscuits

ingredients	Metric	Imperial	American
Soft brown sugar	50 g	2 oz	¼ cup
Peanut butter	50 g	2 oz	¼ cup
Hard butter or margarine	15 ml	1 tbsp	1 tbsp
Egg, beaten	½	½	½
Pinch of bicarbonate of soda (baking soda)			
Pinch of salt			
Few drops of vanilla essence (extract)			
Plain (all-purpose) flour	50 g	2 oz	½ cup
Salted peanuts, chopped	25 g	1 oz	¼ cup

method

1. Mix the sugar, peanut butter, butter or margarine, egg, bicarbonate of soda, salt and vanilla essence and beat until light and fluffy.

2. Stir in the flour and peanuts. Shape the dough into a roll and cut into 5 mm/¼ in slices.

3. Arrange the slices on a baking sheet lined with greaseproof (waxed) paper and microwave on Medium for 1-3 minutes until just dry on the surface.

 6-8 min Preparation time

EASTER BISCUITS

Makes 12 biscuits

ingredients	Metric	Imperial	American
Butter or margarine	75 g	3 oz	6 tbsp
Caster (superfine) sugar	75 g	3 oz	6 tbsp
Egg, beaten	1	1	1
Plain (all-purpose) flour	175 g	6 oz	1½ cups
Currants	50 g	2 oz	⅓ cup
Mixed spice	2.5 ml	½ tsp	½ tsp
Glaze:			
Egg white	1	1	1
Caster (superfine) sugar	15 ml	1 tbsp	1 tbsp

method

1. Cream the butter or margarine and sugar. Mix in the egg and fold in the flour, currants and spice to make a firm dough.

2. Roll out the dough on a lightly floured surface and cut into 7.5 cm/3 in rounds.

3. Arrange 6 biscuits on greaseproof (waxed) paper and microwave on High for 2 minutes. Brush with egg white and sprinkle with caster sugar and microwave on High for a further 1 minute.

4. Repeat with the remaining biscuits.

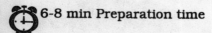 6-8 min Preparation time

COCONUT COOKIES

ingredients	Metric	Imperial	American
Soft margarine	25 g	1 oz	2 tbsp
Sugar	25 g	1 oz	2 tbsp
Small egg, beaten	½	½	½
Drop of vanilla essence			
Plain (all-purpose) flour	40 g	1½ oz	5 tbsp
Desiccated (shredded) coconut	15 ml	1 tbsp	1 tbsp
Raspberry jam	15 ml	1 tbsp	1 tbsp

method

1. Beat together the margarine and sugar until light. Stir in the egg and vanilla then mix in the flour and coconut. Knead to a smooth dough.

2. Divide the dough into 8 and shape into balls. Press a handle into each one to make a hollow. Arrange on a plate lined with microwave film and microwave on High for 3-4 minutes until just firm.

3. Spoon a little jam into the centre of each cookie and leave to cool.

 6-8 min Preparation time

CHEESE BISCUITS

Makes about 48 biscuits suitable for freezing before baking

ingredients	Metric	Imperial	American
Strong Cheddar cheese, grated	175 g	6 oz	1½ cups
Plain (all-purpose) flour	75 g	3 oz	¾ cup
Wholewheat flour	75 g	3 oz	¾ cup
Butter or margarine	175 g	6 oz	¾ cup
Caraway seeds	5 ml	1 tsp	1 tsp
Few drops of tabasco sauce			
Gruyère cheese, grated	50 g	2 oz	½ cup
Pinch of paprika			

method

1. Mix the Cheddar cheese, flours, butter or margarine, caraway seeds and tabasco sauce in a medium sized bowl and beat until well blended.

2. Roll out on a floured surface to a thickness of 3 mm/⅛ in. Cut out with small biscuits cutters. Sprinkle with Gruyère cheese and paprika.

3. Arrange a few biscuits at a time on a baking sheet and microwave on High for 3-6 minutes until the biscuits appear dry, rearranging 2 or 3 times. Leave to stand for 1 minute. Cool on a wire rack.

4. Continue with the remaining biscuits.

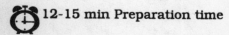 12-15 min Preparation time

NUTTY ICE CREAM DESSERT

ingredients	Metric	Imperial	American
Plain (all-purpose) flour	25 g	1 oz	2 tbsp
Brown sugar	15 ml	1 tbsp	1 tbsp
Chopped mixed nuts	15 ml	1 tbsp	1 tbsp
Butter or margarine, cubed	25 g	1 oz	2 tbsp
Vanilla ice cream	300 ml	½ pt	1¼ cups
Golden syrup	15 ml	1 tbsp	1 tbsp
Dry roasted peanuts	15 ml	1 tbsp	1 tbsp
Whipped cream	30 ml	2 tbsp	2 tbsp

method

1. Mix the flour, sugar and nuts. Blend in the butter or margarine to form coarse crumbs then press the mixture against the bottom and sides of an individual pie plate. Microwave on Medium for 2-3 minutes until dry and firm. Leave to cool.

2. Spoon the ice cream over the base and spoon the syrup over the top. Sprinkle with peanuts and top with whipped cream.

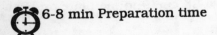 6-8 min Preparation time

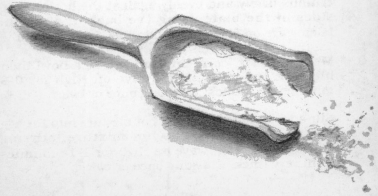

CHOCOLATE FUDGE TART

Makes 2 x 23 cm/9 in tarts suitable for freezing before decorating with whipped cream.

ingredients	Metric	Imperial	American
Crust:			
Butter or margarine	75 g	3 oz	6 tbsp
Digestive biscuit (Graham cracker) crumbs	150 g	5 oz	1¼ cups
Brown or granulated sugar	50 g	2 oz	¼ cup
Filling:			
Sugar	100 g	4 oz	½ cup
Cornflour (cornstarch)	30 ml	2 tbsp	2 tbsp
Salt	2.5 ml	½ tsp	½ tsp
Milk	400 ml	14 fl oz	1¾ cups
Egg yolks	4	4	4
Plain chocolate chips	150 g	5 oz	1¼ cups
Vanilla essence (extract)	2.5 ml	½ tsp	½ tsp
Coffee liqueur	45 ml	3 tbsp	3 tbsp
Whipped cream	250 ml	8 fl oz	1 cup

method

1. Melt the butter in a 23 cm/9 in pie plate on High for 45-60 seconds.

2. Stir in the biscuit crumbs and sugar. Press the crumbs firmly and evenly against the bottom and sides of the plate, using the back of a spoon. Microwave on High for 1½ minutes. Leave to cool.

3. Mix the sugar, cornflour and salt in a bowl then blend in the milk. Microwave on High for 6-9 minutes until thick, whisking once or twice.

4. Stir a small amount of the hot mixture into the egg yolks. Return it to the hot mixture, stirring constantly. Microwave on High for 1-1½ minutes until very thick, whisking once or twice.

5. Stir in the chocolate chips until they melt, then the vanilla essence. Pour into the crust and chill until set.

6. Blend the liqueur into the whipped cream and spread on the cooled filling.

16-20 min Preparation time plus chilling

INDEX